HOW TO HELP THE HURTING

*When Friends Face Problems
with Self-Esteem, Self-Control,
Fear, Depression, Loneliness*

Everett L. Worthington, Jr.

INTERVARSITY PRESS
DOWNERS GROVE, ILLINOIS 60515

InterVarsity Press is the book-publishing division of Inter-Varsity Christian Fellowship, a student movement active on campus at hundreds of universities, colleges and schools of nursing. For information about local and regional activities, write IVCF, 233 Langdon St., Madison, WI 53703.

Distributed in Canada through InterVarsity Press, 860 Denison St., Unit 3, Markham, Ontario L3R 4H1, Canada.

Quotations from the Bible, unless otherwise noted, are taken from the Revised Standard Version of the Bible, copyrighted 1946, 1952, © 1971, 1973. Those marked NIV are taken from the Holy Bible, New International Version. Copyright © 1973, 1978, International Bible Society. Used by permission of Zondervan Bible Publishers. Those quoted in figure 6 on page 107 are from The Living Bible, copyright © 1971 by Tyndale House Publishers, Wheaton, Illinois.

Cover photograph: Michael Goss

ISBN 0-87784-388-0

Printed in the United States of America

Library of Congress Cataloging in Publication Data
Worthington, Everett L., 1946-
   How to help the hurting.

   Bibliography: p.
   1. Peer counseling in the church.   I. Title.
BV4409.W66   1985   253.5   85-23070
ISBN 0-87784-388-0

17	16	15	14	13	12	11	10	9	8	7	6	5	4	3	2	1
99	98	97	96	95	94	93	92	91	90	89	88	87	86	85		

*To my parents
and
Kirby's parents*

1 WHO, ME? HELP OTHERS? *13*

2 I'M JUST A TOAD *21*

3 IMPROVING SELF-IMAGE *33*

4 WANTED: SELF-CONTROL *43*

5 WINNING THE BATTLE FOR SELF-CONTROL *53*

6 THE TYRANNY OF FEAR *69*

7 CALMING THE FEARFUL *77*

8 DEPRESSION: A DOWNWARD SPIRAL *91*

9 HELPING THE DEPRESSED *101*

10 THE PAIN OF LONELINESS *119*

11 DEFEATING LONELINESS *127*

12 HELPING IN A CRISIS *143*

13 THINE IS THE POWER *153*

APPENDIX *159*

NOTES *165*

Preface

The Spirit of the Lord is upon me,
because he has anointed me to preach good news to the poor.
He has sent me to proclaim release to the captives
and recovering of sight to the blind,
to set at liberty those who are oppressed,
to proclaim the acceptable year of the Lord. Luke 4:18-19

Jesus began his public ministry by sounding the clarion call to help others. Jesus is our example of the living sacrifice, and we too are called to lay down our lives for others. We are the body of Christ. He accomplishes his ministry through us. Because he has gone to the Father and has left his Holy Spirit in us, we will do his work—and even greater works than he did (see Jn 14:12).

This book aims to help you help others. It gives ways to view common psychological problems and offers specific suggestions for helping others overcome their problems. Finally, it shows through actual dialogs how to use the suggestions.

You *can* help your friends. Research has shown that nonprofessional helpers can give excellent counsel. In fact, most counseling done today is done by one friend with another. In many cases this counsel helps people avoid the expense of professional help. By improving your counseling skills you can be a more active part in the healing body of Christ. Sometimes our friends need help beyond what we can safely give. This book is not intended to be a substitute for professional treatment of mental illness or those who are suicidal. The author and the publisher encourage you to seek professional consultation rather than try to help those who are deeply troubled. Although this book should help you give better counsel, it will not—by itself—qualify you to give psychotherapy to the disturbed. Such skills are developed only through the anointing of the Holy Spirit and years of study and supervised experience. Pray for wisdom before you counsel.

In the first part of this book we look at a general model for helping others (chapter one), which was illustrated in detail in *When Someone Asks for Help* (IVP, 1982), and we introduce themes that run throughout the book.

The main body of the book tackles common psychological problems. One of the most common problems is poor self-concept, self-image and self-esteem (chapters two and three). Chapters four and five look at self-control, temptation and impulse control. Their lessons are also applicable to defeating persistent sin. Chapters six and and seven explore fear and anxiety, giving a general method for helping a friend conquer fear. Chapters eight and nine deal with depression, the most prevalent emotional problem in the United States today. Chapters ten and eleven explore the causes and cures of loneliness.

The final chapters focus again on our role as helpers. Chapter twelve discusses helping in times of unexpected, immediate need—a crisis. Chapter thirteen cautions us all about presuming that we can accomplish anything apart from God. It directs our attention to Jesus, the Healer, and affirms the sovereignty of God in governing his creation.

The goals of counseling are to help people experience less psychological pain, to act responsibly to control their lives and to yield themselves to God's care and direction. Personal problems will arise as long as we live in God's world. I hope that this book will give each of us some practical ways to help another find help and answers. May God have the glory.

Acknowledgments

This book grew out of my first book, *When Someone Asks for Help: A Practical Guide for Counseling*. Many of the people who helped with the first project have, in large part, helped with this one too.

Some people, though, have played a special part in helping this book come together. The ideas were developed in two Sunday-school classes—one at Evangelical Free Church in Columbia, Missouri, and the other at Christ Presbyterian Church in Richmond, Virginia. The people in those classes provided not only an impetus to think through how to teach about each problem, but they also gave feedback about some of the ideas. Many in my church community have supported me through prayer and encouragement. I will always be grateful.

Geoff Sutton has provided assistance, particularly with the chapter on loneliness. He has also read and commented on portions of the manuscript. I am indebted to him.

Don Danser, a friend and colleague, has provided support at my work and has shared many ideas and prayers with me during the past few years. In addition, we co-taught the course at Christ Presbyterian Church. Don has been a faith-building inspiration to me.

Rena Canipe has graciously provided a place in Florida for my family to rest and recuperate during the summer months while

I wrote large portions of the manuscript. She has also modeled love and service. Wayne and Sandi Canipe have also endured inconvenience and provided support and encouragement while we have visited in Florida. They each deserve a medal for extraordinary sacrifice.

I extend my thanks to Andy Le Peau, Betsy Elliot and Mickey Maudlin, InterVarsity Press editors who helped improve my writing through their patient attention to detail, meticulous revision of my work, and thoughtful comments about how I could improve. In addition, Martin Bolt critiqued an earlier draft of the manuscript and provided many helpful suggestions for revisions.

Finally, I thank Kirby and our children who have endured long periods hearing the typewriter clackety-clacking behind closed doors. They have given more than any.

The final version of the manuscript for this book was produced by the Information Processing Center, Dean's Office, College of Humanities and Sciences, Virginia Commonwealth University, Gene Dunaway, Supervisor. My thanks also go to Gene, who not only typed the manuscript but also provided comments and encouragement.

1

WHO, ME?
HELP OTHERS?

Betty sits across from you and pours out her woes. She is unhappy, unfulfilled. Her multitude of problems inundates you. She is depressed and anxious and she hates herself. Her tears drop continually onto the front of her blouse. She is looking for help, and frankly you don't know what to do. The futility of her predicament is too real, too powerful. As you think of Betty's feelings, you find that you feel her depression and hopelessness.

You are overwhelmed by questions. Your mind reels, silently shouting condemnation about your own inadequacy as a helper: "What is Betty's real problem? What is causing her pain? How can I help her when it seems that her situation is hopeless? What can I do? What can *she* do? Nothing!"

If you have ever been in a situation like this—frustrated by your inability to help friends in distress—then you know one of the paradoxes of counseling. Helping people with emotional problems depends on understanding them, on tracking their thoughts and feelings, and on making a deep personal connection with them. Yet the more you identify with your friends, think with them and experience their feelings, the less likely you are to break those mindsets and help.

You hear them tell how they have tried numerous solutions. And when their first attempts didn't work, they tried harder. They may have even asked other friends or family for help. But their suggestions didn't work either.

Now they turn to you. They tell you their difficulties—how the problem started, what they have tried to do about it and how each attempt has failed. As you listen, you begin to sense the futility of solving the problem and to feel their own discouragement.

Needed: New Plans and Actions

To help a friend, we must provide a new, objective way to view the problem—one that will lead to new actions that solve the problem. This book aims to help you do just that by examining five of the most common personal problems people face—self-esteem, self-control, anxiety, depression and loneliness.

Armed with new weapons, we can avoid being snared by frustration as we listen to our friends. After we have listened carefully and have understood them thoroughly, we will have some new ideas and plans to fall back on.

Effective helpers follow a five-stage method of helping.

Stage 1. Listening and understanding.

Stage 2. Helping rethink the problem.

Stage 3. Formulating workable action plans.

Stage 4. Supporting the person as the action plans are implemented.

Stage 5. Following up the person with continued love.[1]

As you move through this process, I assume that you are skilled at "joining" with people who have sought your help. You know how to avoid unhelpful communication. You can detect the subtleties of people's emotions through their facial and bodily expressions. You can tell what people want from you and whether you are capable of helping. You can understand their view of their problems and can convey your understanding. Further, you can skillfully help people rethink their problems without their feeling that you are forcing them to accept your way of thinking. And you are able to suggest action plans (once you have them!) in ways that encourage people to put the plans into effect rather than provoke them to resist your suggestions. (If you feel weak in any of these skills, you may want to review *When Someone Asks for Help*.) This book focuses on stages two and three: helping to rethink problems and form new action plans for specific common difficulties.

We *Can* Help

Professionals are not the only people who can give effective counsel. Most effective counseling is done by people just like you.[2] When people have problems, they turn first to their friends and family. With the advice and counsel they receive, most people solve their problems and look no further. The pastor or professional counselor is only sought when the counsel of friends or family does not work.

People, even those without training, often help their friends. Research has shown, though, that lay people can help their friends more effectively if they have had some training.[3] We can't learn to counsel by merely reading a book or attending lectures or classes about counseling. It takes much experience, preferably experience under the supervision of an experienced counselor, to refine helping skills. But we can expand our repertoire of ideas about helping through reading. This book won't turn anyone into a professional, but it can give all of us who would help our friends greater flexibility and effectiveness.

When friends ask for help, usually they expect us to listen and support them. Most do not want advice at first. So an important part of helping is what I call stage one helping—understanding people and communicating that understanding to them. Once they are secure in our support, people are ready for our counsel.

Our effectiveness as a helper depends on our effectiveness as a willing listener and supportive friend.

It feels good to be asked for help. God created us to help, and it is our Christian calling: "Through love be servants of one another" (Gal 5:13). But a couple of warnings are in order. First, we must know our limitations. If we try to help when we are unable, we are not serving. Psychological problems are not simple, and it is often hard for even professionals to determine how severely someone is disturbed. Be careful then to ask continually, "Am I able to help? Would someone else be a more effective helper?"

Have confidence in yourself and in the healing God, but be sensitive to whether God is really calling you to be the instrument of his healing or to be a referral agent. Problems that are stubbornly persistent, that result in extreme emotions and that make people feel as if they have little or no control usually indicate the need for at least a consultation with a professional.

The second warning is in order after we have had some success in helping. It is easy to think that good results in counseling are due to the power of our techniques. Our attention may become focused on what we can say and do to promote healing. But it is crucial to remind ourselves continually that counseling techniques heal no one. Jesus is the healer. A sure way to fail at counseling is to overrely on our skill as a helper. Even if we should succeed at helping, we are ultimately failing both our friends and ourselves in furthering the kingdom of God.

Jesus Christ is the totally sufficient healer, and we are his body. Jesus works through us. Often his work looks miraculous to us— such as when we pray and someone experiences a miracle. Often his work looks mundane to us—such as when we simply meet the daily needs of our children, loving them in a practical way.

Our role as Christian helpers is to prepare ourselves for the mundane work of supporting a friend in need, exerting all of our well-developed helping skills to help the person conquer his or her distress, and praying for God to solve the person's problem. We are responsible for doing everything in our power to promote healing. God is responsible for the healing. Sometimes we will be the instrument through which he heals. Sometimes we will be the instrument through which he loves the person enough to stick with them through years of problems. By developing our helping skills we can be ready when God calls us to put them to use.

People with problems need new perspectives to lead them to new ways of acting. Unfortunately, problems generally trap people into rigid attempts at problem solving. As agents of Jesus we want to help free people from their restrictive problem-solving attempts: "For freedom Christ has set us free" (Gal 5:1). When people are freed to act differently, others respond differently to them and the cycle is broken.

Psychologists call my approach to problems cognitive-behavioral. That is, I try to help people think differently and act more responsibly. This does not mean that I believe people's emotions, bodies and brain chemistry are unimportant. To the contrary, God created people whose entire lives are affected by problems. However, a cognitive-behavioral approach *generally* uses people's thoughts, behaviors and environments to open doorways into their lives. Jesus always met people where they were. He reasoned with Nicodemus. He healed the sick. He told the adulterous woman merely to change her behavior—"Go, and do not sin again" (Jn 8:11). All of these approaches led to relationships with needy people that catapulted them closer to Jesus, to God the Father, and to health.

My approach to psychological problems is to enter people's lives through what they are thinking and doing. My goals are to relieve their distress and enhance their relationship with Jesus.

That Overconfident Feeling

When we know helpful ways to rethink problems, we want to hurry people to see our new perspective. We want to relieve their distress. Yet this desire to *help quickly* may work against us, for it impels us to try to change people before we have "joined" with them. *We must not become so eager to provide a new way of thinking that we stop listening and supporting!* We need to join with people by letting them describe their problems thoroughly, including all their attempts to solve them. We need to show that we care—that we understand just what they have felt and that we feel with them in their struggles.

Sometimes, though, every one of us tries to help too quickly. We get our metaphorical blinders on and charge straight ahead toward our goal, regardless of what the other person does or says. One signal warns me when I am doing this: when I catch myself trying to interrupt people to tell something that I am sure will help, it usually indicates that I am following my agenda rather than theirs. One of my friends, Fred DiBlasio, says that when he begins to make hand gestures while he talks, he knows immediately that he is not listening. Take it as a cue you are moving too quickly if people get suddenly quiet or get more insistent in telling about their problems.

Having a plan that we know works can create a problem. It makes us reluctant to believe that the plan will not work with our friends. Unfortunately, no counseling plan always works. Some people need help from those with more experience in dealing with certain types of problems. It is better to err by requesting help unnecessarily than by not seeking a consultation when it is needed.

As you try out the methods I suggest in this book (or any other, for that matter), you will experience both successes and failures. Early success can breed pride if you do not give the glory to God. Early failure can lead to despair, which is perhaps more common. *We must walk the fence between pride and despair.* Helping people conquer psychological problems takes persistence, prayer and patience. We want people to respond instantly to our help, but they usually don't. Helping is an act of love. It takes perseverance.

One look at the Bible should show us that God acts uniquely with each person. He does not always confront, nor does he always act gently. Sometimes his love is tough, sometimes tender. If God is so varied with his help, let that teach us. There are many ways to help. We have no corner on "God's way."

Human difficulties are problems to solve. Let us be courageous enough to take the most promising approach we have available to solve a problem rather than try to use the same approach for all problems. We need not be afraid to take risks, to experiment. There are many ways to build a highway through a desert. Many different solutions to the same problem will work, not just one. But each solution requires that we work intimately with the person, investing our time and energy.

As we live within a body of Christians, we will have many opportunities to minister to others and to be ministered to in our need. We too will accept help from others, glad for the chance to allow them to sacrifice their time and energy and even material resources for us. Christianity is believing, having faith, loving and living in that sacrificial love that Jesus spreads throughout his body. We are always ready to help, both in crises and in long-term relationships with those in need.

2

I'M JUST
A TOAD

No matter what I did, I could never please my father," Joan said. "Now I'm thirty-nine. He's been dead for years, and I can't please anyone. I'm just a toad, a worthless toad."

Joan's comment, taken from an actual counseling tape, summarizes how many people feel about themselves.* Why do problems with the self so often cripple people for life?

"My work was once interesting," complained Joan, "but now it seems as if case after case just crawls across my desk, almost unnoticed, and dies forgotten in my 'out' basket. I don't get involved with the people I'm supposed to be helping at the bank. It's just day after day of the same thing. I can do my job without even thinking about it, but sometimes I wonder if I *could* do anything else. I know that there must be thousands of jobs that I would find more challenging and fulfilling, but I can't seem to

---

* Names and circumstances of people have been changed to protect their identity.

get motivated to go look for them.

"I don't really have any friends either. My parents are dead, and my only brother lives in Wisconsin, so I never see him. About five years ago Franklin and I had lots of friends. Then, after our divorce, they all seemed to melt into the woodwork—except for Brenda and Cloe. But, with the house and the demands of the job . . . well, I never seem to have much time for them. That house is an albatross around my neck. There's always something to do. If it isn't inside work, it's outside. It's a prison. It is, a real prison. I can't get free to be with either Brenda or Cloe. Cloe never seems to have any time, and Brenda . . . Well, you really can tell who your friends are when the chips are down. She says she can't stand the 'emotional investment' of being with me 'cause I'm 'always complaining,' *she* says, and never willing to do anything about it.

"And church is no help," Joan went on. "It's dull. I hardly ever go anymore—maybe once a month. Nobody cares. Why should they? I'm worthless. Just a toad. What good is a toad to anyone?"

A Sense of Worth

Like all of us, Joan is struggling for a sense of who she is and for a sense of worth.[1] She is unhappy. She looks for meaning in two areas—competence in her work and intimacy in her friendships. Since the Garden of Eden, all of us have had these two fundamental needs. One of the first things God did for Adam was to get him cultivating the garden, establishing meaningful work for him (Gen 2:7-9, 15). Then God made Eve his helper (Gen 2:18). Both could achieve some sense of worth through the work God had provided. And both could also be in relationship, first with God and then with each other (Gen 1:26-27; 2:18, 24). At the heart of both the old and the new covenants is the need for our roles in work and in relationships to function properly.

Joan has deficiencies in both areas. Her work has lost any fulfilling role because she has let it become routine. Enthusiasm has given way to boredom, learning to routine performance. Her loss of interest seems to have sprung more from her general malaise with life than from the job itself. Her motivation has been leeched out by failing to look for the new, the original, in each of her projects. Work is not rewarding. She feels empty.

Her relationships too are bankrupt. After her divorce, Joan suffered the normal loneliness that occurs when any great upheaval takes place, whether death, divorce, career change, retirement or moving. Old personal ties are severed, and new lines must be tossed to others. But Joan dwelt on her negative feelings and circumstances. She not only failed to establish new ties, but she weakened her remaining friendships to mere threads through her frequent complaining.

Her faith, which was never strong, brought her no comfort. Joan pulled away from church fellowship. She began to doubt whether God cared. This left her with what Pascal once called a God-shaped vacuum—an empty spot in her life that only God could fill.

Many of Joan's troubles traced back to early rejection. People rejected her, and she rejected them and God. Rejection is often at the core of problems with self-worth.

Jesus, who was like us in every way except that he did not sin, was rejected and killed, but he rose triumphant. Because he rose, we can conquer even the most cruel rejections.[2] But victory isn't automatic. If we respond to rejection by holding on to resentment and anger, we breed trouble.

Resentment and anger, left alone, give rise to bitterness, which can take root in us and poison us. Bitterness can lead to hate, fear of further rejection, an unhealthy craving for love, for acceptance and attention at any price, and the need to be right—to please people and to succeed at all costs. These fruits of bitterness show up in our behavior. When we fear that people will reject us again, we begin to withdraw, to isolate ourselves, and to become "hard" or defensive. Fearing rejection at work, we may begin to procrastinate, lose our ambition, or even become chronically unemployed. These behaviors in turn make us feel guilty and lead us to a cycle of self-justification for the way we're acting.

Feeding the Rejection Cycle

Bitterness turns us inward. We become self-preoccupied and we reject others. We experience lowered self-esteem, a poor self-concept and a damaged self-image. This causes more rejection from others, which leads to more bitterness. Thus the cycle feeds itself.[3]

How do we help break that cycle?

We start with current behavior. No matter how problems with the self began, if they are still causing trouble, the current behavior is to blame. It is maintaining the problem. People try to cope with their difficulties, but in coping they sometimes create problems even harder to correct than the original ones. They may even deepen their sense of worthlessness.

We want to help people find the part of life that is reinforcing a low self-esteem. That is the first step. We can generally look for current triggers for self-doubt in three areas—people's actions, beliefs and circumstances (A-B-C).[4]

Actions. Inadequate social skills, poor work behaviors and persistent sin commonly feed problems with the self. Ask yourself whether the person lacks the ability to make and keep friends, lacks the opportunity to meet friends, or has merely arranged life in a way that leaves little time to spend with friends. Observe recurring kinds of behavior that repel people, like complaining, arguing, using sarcasm, acting aggressively, dominating or sabotaging attempts to help. Acting like this is costly, extracting its toll even among loyal friends.

If the person can't find meaning in work, look for signs of procrastination. Does he fail to make important decisions or take risks? Does he make poor judgment calls on the job? Does he have the skills and interest needed to perform well? Not all work difficulties are solely the responsibility of the individual you are trying to help. Some (or all) might be uncontrollable. It may be that the job simply demands too much or too little. But we can help a friend determine where the problem lies.

Persistent sin is the third factor that erodes a self-concept. Peter Marshall once said, "You can't do wrong and feel right."[5] One tempting sin for a person who has problems with the self is emotional self-indulgence—in anger, criticism, bitterness or self-pity. These sins are particularly insidious because people become "friends" with them, cherishing their feelings. God won't deliver people from their friends. He requires that they first see sin with his eyes and turn from it. We can help friends see what God sees in their current actions.

Beliefs. People need to know where they stand. Sometimes problems come from their not understanding their relationship to God (or others). We know that in God's sight people are worthwhile. Even before they knew God, Jesus was willing to die for them. After people know Jesus, they can rest assured that they are new creatures and temples of the living God. People have value. God's Word tells us so.

Yet people can know these truths and still feel miserable. If Christians doubt their worth, it may be because they misunderstand their relationship to Jesus. Maybe they know him as their savior and priest, but not as their King and Lord. When we isolate areas of our lives from the lordship of Jesus, we discover our own inadequacies. Sins of omission rather than commission generally characterize those who haven't given Jesus full control. They neglect people and fail at the law of love.

People might also feel inadequate because of contamination from the world. Adopting prevalent beliefs, such as the adequacy of humans apart from God or the absence of any absolute truths, leads to despair when people fall on their faces in failure. Distorted beliefs lead to distorted thinking. One unfortunate way of thinking in some Christian circles is to see everything in black or white. People or ideas are either for me or against me, right or wrong, good or bad. This thinking is an exaggeration of biblical teaching, a perversion of the truth. Some things *are* absolute. Many are not. We must learn to discern which is which.

A rigid way of thinking often supports a poor self-concept. For example, a single happening is stretched into a general rule: a single failure turns into the belief that *I am* a failure. Discouraged people tend to interpret small actions to support their already-negative beliefs about themselves. Curtis believed he was totally undesirable to women. When a woman that he knew complimented him for having "warm and tender eyes," he became depressed. Since he already knew he was undesirable to women, he knew that this woman was making fun of him by her compliment. By this reasoning Curtis maintained his poor self-concept, even twisting the evidence that should have changed his mind about himself. Such reasoning is more common than one might think: people often prefer the misery of the known to the terror of the unfamiliar. They become comfortable with a low self-image.

Once negative beliefs about the self exist, the mind continually reindoctrinates itself with "proof." Negative, self-downing, self-destructive thoughts often run wild through the mind, like enemy soldiers running through a conquered city, leaving carnage in their wake. "You're no good. You're worthless," a person chants like a mantra. Minds become propaganda machines, churning out emotional claptrap to defeat the inner person. Engaged in a cold war of the mind, the person feeds depression with every defeat and even, through mental trickery, every success.

Most people also think in visual terms. Many develop an image, a picture of themselves or their circumstances. For example, a woman once told me, "I feel like every day the world is putting poison in my food." Such a metaphor can become a script, like the script in a play, that governs action. One man might play "the rejected one." A woman might be "always misunderstood." Such scripts, such pictures of ourselves as warriors, princesses or even garbage, propel our behavior—toward healing or toward illness.[6] We need to help people choose to follow a new script; but first they must realize the self-fulfilling predictions they have created.

Circumstances. Self-doubt is only natural when our world really is giving us a hard time. If a woman continually bumps into or works with critical, nonaffirming people, it is not surprising that she adopts some of their attitudes. Persistent failure in business, child rearing or relationships can cause anyone to become introspective and self-questioning. Often people can do little about these circumstances. As helpers, we must try to discern whether this is the case. When we listen to troubled people describe their woes, we get a one-sided picture. We can, however, help them explore what actions might improve a difficult situation, and we can help them assess how much improvement they can realistically hope for.

A final circumstance that might precipitate problems with the self is spiritual warfare. How we act has effects in the unseen world. Faith overcomes Satan and his legions; unbelief gives them power. Similarly, actions of angels and (unfortunately) demons can affect our lives. The Holy Spirit helps us discern spiritual activity (1 Cor 12:8-10). If we would be effective helpers, we should earnestly desire this spiritual gift. Perhaps a gentle nudge will prompt us to pray for another's spiritual protection. Perhaps it will merely seem right for us to enter active spiritual warfare on behalf of the other. We must discern his leading and then follow.

Helping Joan
Beset by a poor self-concept, self-image and self-esteem, Joan needs help. She needs the understanding, support and acceptance of another person. She must be helped to understand how she was maintaining her destructive view of herself.

Darla talked with Joan over a period of time. Because Darla was an experienced counselor, the excerpted interviews given here show us how we can help people explore the current causes of their distress. By now we are familiar with some of the hypotheses that Darla holds about Joan's problems. Observe *how* she helps Joan become aware of the hypotheses and test them out. The same techniques will help you help a friend.

Joan: I know that a lot of my problems are because I never

| | could please my father. I know it. But it doesn't help me to know it. I keep feeling so inadequate. I keep feeling so depressed and disappointed with myself. I just don't know what to do about it. |

Darla: I can see how much it upsets you to think about it. You're frustrated and it feels absolutely hopeless.

Joan: It does.

Darla: Even now, as you describe your frustration, it seems to push you deeper into the mire.

Joan: It does. I get depressed thinking about it.

Darla: When was the last time you got depressed?

Joan began by offering an invitation for Darla to *do something*. She said that she did not know what to do about her feelings of inadequacy. It would have been easy for Darla to offer suggestions, but Darla understood that she knew too little about the current forces maintaining Joan's feelings of inadequacy. Suspecting that Joan is reindoctrinating herself continually with negative thinking, Darla uses Joan's feelings as a springboard. She wants Joan to explore how her thoughts maintain her poor self-esteem.

Joan: Last night was bad.

Darla: What started it?

Joan: A TV show, kind of a love story. I was half paying attention as I folded clothes, but I got hooked. Then afterwards, I looked down and found that I had only half of the clothes folded. I got really mad at myself then.

Darla: You must have got mad for a reason. Were you thinking something or imagining something? Try to remember exactly what was going on in your mind as you sat there.

Joan: I guess I thought, "Now I've done it. I've wasted the whole night watching that stupid show. And all it did was get me depressed."

Darla: What else?

Joan: You know, the same old thing I always think.

Darla: Tell me. Pretend you are thinking aloud, right now.

Joan: Well, my mind just goes from topic to topic—all of them depressing.

Joan seems reluctant to discuss her thoughts. Perhaps they are embarrassing. For whatever reason, though, Darla must help Joan overcome her inhibitions about revealing her thoughts. She cannot make progress if thoughts are described in vague sentences.

Darla: It's probably hard to remember all that went through your mind, but, Joan, I think it might help to try to recall it. My guess is that your thoughts are some of the prime culprits that keep you so down on yourself. If you don't examine those thoughts in the light of reason, it will be hard to change them.

Joan: You might be right. I always seem to think the same old records.

Darla: Would you like to play one of those records now in a pretend-type setting?

Joan: Okay. I guess I thought, "How come I always get sucked into these worthless TV shows? I'm the weakest-willed person in the world. I don't think there's any hope." I'm so undisciplined. I just torture myself with these love stories, knowing that I'll never have anyone to love me. No, that's not true. Somebody might love me, sometime. Huh! Oh, I don't know. It's crazy to think about it, though. I know that. It's torture. Why do I torture myself? I must love to abuse myself. What a toad. Just a stupid, ugly, good-for-nothing toad! Look. This is the way it always ends—with me calling myself names. It's depressing.

Darla: I know that was hard for you, and I admire your courage in going through with it. I think there is a lot there to work with, though. It's like brainwashing. You get in a vulnerable condition, and then a record is played over and over in your mind. In your weakened state there is almost no recourse but to believe the record.

Joan: That's the way it seems.

Darla's persistence paid off. Joan opened up. Before accepting those thoughts as typical, however, Darla tried to check it out in other circumstances. For two sessions they explored Joan's thinking. Between the two sessions Darla asked Joan to keep an informal "thought diary," in which she recorded what she thought about when she became depressed. Although Joan only completed the thought diary two times during the week, it helped convince her that her thoughts were affecting her moods, and it provided a treasure house of possibilities for change during the later parts of counseling.

Guidelines for Helping

People with self-doubts have usually had them for a long time. The doubts might have only recently flared to problem proportion, but the difficulty has been long present. The person often has a history of perceived rejection and may have tried numerous ways to cope with his or her inadequacies. Often the person is stuck, realizing that the problem is with the self but not knowing if anything can ever be done about it. With the problems often come depression, hopelessness, anger and skill deficits, so that they are riveted into place by present behavior.

As a helper who is trying to understand people, consider the following guidelines:

1. Support your friends through difficult trials. Encourage them to turn to Jesus and to continue trying to make changes.

2. Affirm what you know that is positive about them, based on Scripture and on your dealing with them.

3. Accept their thoughts, feelings and behaviors. Try to understand them from their point of view. Later you will gently challenge sinful behavior. If people feel that you understand, they will be likely to heed your challenges rather than rebel against them and you.

4. Listen to what they say. Take them seriously. Don't try to reassure them that no problem exists.

5. Be patient. Your most effective helping might be simple human understanding and acceptance.

6. Pray for guidance about how you can help. Seek the spiritual gift of discernment to detect possible spiritual warfare.

7. Be specific as you attempt to learn what is happening in their life. Do not accept vague descriptions as the whole story. Be firm and loving in pursuing details, but do not push so hard that you drive them away.

8. Do not expect simple answers. Even if we clearly understand the cause of the problem, all we've done is to clear the way for hard work. It's not easy to eliminate current causes. Solving the problem is not as simple as merely getting people to see that they really are worthwhile. Past healings and present changes must be made before people can live happily, with meaning.

9. Do not be dismayed if people reject your help or even you. If they do, keep offering love and support, and offer help only tentatively until trust is re-established.

Following these guidelines will not guarantee that we will understand people, but it will give the Holy Spirit opportunity to minister love and compassion to the person through us. It will prepare people for future suggestions about what they can do to defeat problems with the self.

3
IMPROVING SELF-IMAGE

You were rejected," said Darla, "not just once, but again and again. No matter what you did, you could always see your father's lips tighten and the little muscle in his jaw set. Disapproval. Disappointment. Disgust. You could read them all in his face."

Joan shifted her position, and a tear tumbled off her cheek. She sat rigidly in front of Darla, eyes closed, remembering the pain.

"Now you are in a room, face to face with him. He still has that disapproving look on his face, and you cringe inside as his eyes stare at you. You can almost cut the tension between the two of you. You want to apologize . . . if only you knew what you had done to offend him so. Maybe it's just being you, something you can't help. It seems so unfair.

"You've been angry at him for years, for his constant disapproval. You know you should forgive him for the hurts, but you can't. You stand rooted to the spot. Pinned by anger and hurt. How can you forgive him?

"There's a knock at the door, and a man steps inside. He faces your father. Although you cannot see his face, you know it is Jesus."

Joan's head bobbed involuntarily.

" 'I have been hurt,' he says to your father. 'Your rejection of your daughter has driven the very nails into my hands. I forgive you.'

"You hear your own voice crack, 'I forgive you too.'

"Ashamed, your father says simply, 'I'm sorry that I hurt you.' You long to rush into his embrace, but before you can move, Jesus turns to face you."

Joan's head bowed in an attitude of surrender.

"Jesus looks straight at you now. At last he says, 'You too have hurt me.' A thousand justifications struggle to escape your lips, but they are overwhelmed by the desire to rush across the room and throw yourself at the feet of Jesus.

" 'I'm sorry I've been bitter and unforgiving,' you blurt out, knowing exactly how you have hurt him.

"You wish to plead for his forgiveness, but before you utter another sound, he says, 'It is forgiven. Don't take back the bitterness from which you are now free.' Then you find yourself kneeling in front of your Lord, hugging his knees and kissing his spotless garment. You are side by side with your father at the feet of Jesus."

Healing of Rejection

Darla narrated this fantasy prayer for Joan. Through Darla's imagination, Joan felt her bondage to bitterness and unforgivingness broken. "Whatever you loose on earth shall be loosed in heaven" (Mt 16:19). After forgiving her father in her imagination, Joan was able to ask Jesus directly for forgiveness. This loosing has the power to heal memories. Ruth Carter Stapleton described it as inner healing by a God who is the master of time, who can repair damages even within our deep past.[1]

Imagined scenes of forgiveness and restitution have countless times opened the way for powerful healings of the self. Using it in the counseling office, in our worship service when elders pray for individuals of the congregation (Jas 5:13-16), and in the living room of our home has convinced me that Jesus can work amazing things through it.

Helpers participate in these healings through narrating the fantasy, and those who are helped participate through activating their own imaginations. But there is no healing apart from Jesus Christ in his finished work on Calvary. Whether he heals instantly or gradually, through helpers or without them, his healing is the miracle.

As helpers, we must firmly brand this dual fact in our minds: Jesus heals; we pray. People with a wounded self need our prayers. We can help them read books about the self. We can recommend lecturers or cassette tapes or conferences. We may even be able to help them see something about the causes of their problem or what maintains it. But this knowledge is worth little without the healing of Jesus. He is the source of life and health. He hears our prayers and answers. People merely accept the healing.

A student in architecture, so the story goes, entered a nationwide contest for building design. Judged by a panel of architects, her design received Honorable Mention. She was utterly depressed. She believed she had the best design. At lunch on the last day of the convention she was sitting over her uneaten sandwich, looking at her creation. An old man was looking at it too. At last he remarked, not knowing who had designed the building, "This one, I think, is the best of the lot." Judges had merely given her work Honorable Mention, but one old man had liked it. The young student went home elated. Why? Because the old man was Frank Lloyd Wright, probably the greatest architect of the time.

If *the* authority tells us something, we can rely on it.

God is *the* authority on who we are. He is our Father, our Creator. He has given us in the Bible his opinion about our worth. We are the redeemed. We are the ransomed. We are worth the blood of God's one and only Son. We are temples of the living

God. If God is for us, who can be against us?

This is good news indeed. Yet many hear this good news and even believe it and still are nagged by problems of self-esteem. Is it because they don't *really* believe God? That answer is too simple. Rather, simply knowing in our minds who we are in Christ does not always cure problems with the self. To help someone change his view of self, we must try to provoke changes in his *non*rational thoughts and images, too. Rarely does the simple and glorious truth that we are the redeemed of God solve all problems in the self.

Defeating Self-Defeat

Particularly misleading is the self-defeating, negative thinking that maintains a damaged self. Because the thoughts are verbal, we are tempted to think we can attack them rationally. But it won't work. These thoughts are by nature irrational. They come automatically and continually. People beset by continual negative self-indoctrination are in the grip of an irrational thought process.

To help defeat these thoughts, help people reprogram their thinking with thoughts that are more edifying. Change comes about in three steps: (1) *recognizing negative thinking,* (2) *interrupting it* and (3) *replacing it with positive thinking.*[2] This three-step routine requires constant practice, especially after the newness wears off, which it does with amazing speed.

Most people have become aware of the negative chatter incessantly rebounding through their mind and have tried unsuccessfully to change it. By now they have given up hope. They do not believe it is possible to change. We must overcome their discouragement before people will be receptive to suggestions. Follow along as Darla continues her talks with Joan.

Joan: What you said last week about brainwashing myself is true. I do it all the time.

Darla: All the time?

Joan: You know, whenever I get down on myself for being no good. This week I kept a record, like you suggested, and wrote down some of the thoughts I was having when I felt the worst. I do a lot of brainwashing. Something will usually set me off—it doesn't take much—and then, when I'm upset and vulnerable, I hear myself talking junk to myself.

Darla: Sounds like you really paid attention to your thoughts this week.

Joan: Well, I only wrote it down a couple of times, but I did pay a lot of attention.

Darla: Let's see what you wrote. Did you bring your thought diary?

Joan: Yeah, I have it right here . . .

(They look together at the negative thoughts that Joan had recorded.)

Joan: I see how I get down, and I see how I really ought to change those thoughts about myself. But, well, I don't know . . .

Darla: What is making you hesitate?

Joan: Well, I've tried to change my thoughts before, and it seems like it really didn't work.

Darla: Do you remember when you tried to do this?

Joan: Actually, I tried this week, and I just couldn't make it work. I would try, but the old negative thoughts just kept coming back. I really don't think it will work very well.

Darla: You might be right, Joan. It doesn't work for everyone. It will be interesting to see whether it works for you. Right now, it doesn't sound as if you have given it a full test. How long do you think you've been brainwashing yourself with negative thinking?

Joan: About all my life.

Darla: How reasonable is it to expect that you can try for one week to make some changes and then find that you never think another negative thought?

Joan: Doesn't sound too reasonable, does it? I must admit:

	it wasn't like I tried continually all week. I really only tried a couple of times.
Darla:	Good. You recognize that it is going to take lots of practice before you can change a lifelong pattern of thinking. You have to be very systematic. Catch yourself thinking negative, interrupt the negative thoughts, and replace them with positive thoughts. Do this over and over again.
Joan:	It sounds so, so artificial.
Darla:	It is artificial. It's like breaking your arm. What happens when you break your arm?
Joan:	You go to the doctor who puts a cast on it.
Darla:	Right. But having your arm in a cast is artificial, isn't it?
Joan:	Uh-huh.
Darla:	That's the way it is when you systematically replace negative thinking with positive thinking. It's like a cast—a device to let your mind heal, but it is artificial while the healing is taking place.
Joan:	I understand. I'll give it a try, I guess.
Darla:	Good. Look at it as an experiment. Give it a fair try and see if it works for you.

New Image for a New Self

People with poor self-esteem generally live in a bleak world. Even their bodies are affected. Their brain produces neurochemicals associated with sadness and despair. Their friends come to expect emotional ordeals when they are with them. They withdraw and often have less fun and get fewer rewards than people with higher self-esteem. How can we help reverse this pattern?

The most direct route to the nonrational part of people's brains is via a nonrational approach. For example, help people praise God for being the way he or she is. Paul declares, "Always and for everything giving thanks in the name of our Lord Jesus Christ to God the Father" (Eph 5:20). It is not reasonable to give thanks *for* having poor self-esteem. But God, the original psychologist, knows the bodies he created for us. He prescribes praise and thanksgiving as the medication for emotional upheaval.

If people find it hard to get going in praise, suggest they start reading the Psalms and helpful books that instruct in praise. Also recommend that they attend prayer and praise services, revivals or special conferences. Consider having prayer and praise with just you and the person participating. All of us are to be tuned to praise: "Rejoice always, pray constantly, give thanks in all circumstances; for this is the will of God in Christ Jesus for you" (1 Thess 5:16-17).

Images are shorthand ways people describe themselves or their circumstances.[3] Because they are nonverbal, images are more difficult to identify than the destructive thinking that eats away the self-concept.

People can change their self-images, however. They must build a new image. It's almost impossible to eliminate an already existing image without replacing it with something else. They can do this by adding to or modifying their old image, or they can create an entirely new image. Either way, they must practice visualizing the new image until it becomes more habitual than the old.

The first step is to figure out how people image themselves. We must listen to them. For example, Joan frequently described herself as a worthless toad. When asked why she called herself a toad, she mentioned her (slightly) bug eyes, her splotchy complexion, her long legs and short torso, and her sharp tongue (attributed to her by her parents). She also believed that she was worth little, good for merely sitting in the middle of a pond all day, doing nothing. This metaphor for Joan included her body image, some past parental labels and an evaluation of her worth—a powerful image.

The second step is to decide whether the metaphor can be changed and, if so, how. For example, Darla helped Joan modify this picture. She had her write a two-page essay on the worth of frogs and toads. Joan spent an hour in the library reading up on frogs and toads. This assignment was perfect for Joan, who was an excellent writer.

Ann Kiemel in her book *I'm Out to Change My World* tells how she helped someone change a poor self-image for a better metaphor.[4] Visiting a neighbor on a routine errand, Ann spontaneously told her that God loved her. Touched, the old woman showed Ann a picture of weeds, saying that all her life she had felt like a weed, always growing where it was not supposed to be. The next morning, Sunday, Ann rousted a florist from his sleep and sent the lady the first bouquet of flowers she had ever had in her house. This symbol of love changed the old lady's self-image dramatically. She was not a weed. She was a flower.

Earlier I mentioned a woman who saw herself as being daily fed food that was poisoned. I replied, "You can't stop people from putting poison in your food. Bad things are always going to happen. All you can do is learn to take the antidote before the poison makes you ill." That metaphor became the plan for her treatment. She learned to cope with the trials that came her way.

If you can think of no way to modify the metaphor, encourage people to create new images for themselves. Explore their positive fantasies and see if a metaphor can be constructed around them. Develop the image in detail. Make it live. Get them to describe what is around the image, the details of the scene. Have them introduce action into the image so that they see themselves as people who are active.

Once the image is fully developed, help people practice it. Avoid having them set aside a time especially to practice. It rarely works. Life's daily routine will soon overwhelm it. (This is why it is often hard for a person to begin to have a quiet time of devotions and prayer if that has not previously been part of the person's daily routine.) Rather, for imagery practice have people select an activity that is done routinely but is boring and repetitive—times like traveling to and from work, washing dishes, mowing the yard, folding clothes or doing household cleaning. Instead of being crowded out of a busy schedule, these activities are already firmly entrenched in the schedule and serve as reminders to practice the new self-image.

Some years ago I wanted to become one who could freely express praise to the Lord. I had always been somewhat inhibited about raising my hands and praising him. It seemed such a simple thing to do: lift them up and praise! But whenever I tried it, I felt that heavy lead was weighting my hands, and when I at last strained them toward heaven, I thought everyone in church must be staring at me. It did little good to admonish myself with Scripture ("I desire then that in every place the men should pray, lifting holy hands"—1 Tim 2:8). Clearly, what I needed was a change in my self-image from a reserved person to a man who could worship the Lord openly and not be concerned with what others thought.

That was the goal. How did I do it? Each day I ride my bicycle eight miles to and from work. That gave me about an hour each day to practice my new image. I began small. I tried to modify my shadow as I rode along. I would imagine my shadow with arms outstretched, face turned to heaven, singing praises to God. (With my singing, neighbors could be glad it was just a shadow.) When I had my shadow trained, I worked on my body, singing praises loudly on back streets. At last I ventured onto the main streets. After numerous quizzical looks from drivers at traffic lights and an "Amen, brother!" from a street preacher, it now seems nothing to raise my hands and sing praises in church.

Hope for a Growing Self

Which comes first—changes in the self or changes in our behavior? The answer is either. And either drives the other. They depend on each other. Behavior change is often the key to changes in the self, just as sometimes changes in our self-concept will help change behavior.

A psychologist named George Kelly developed a way to change the self through changing behavior.[5] Kelly had people write a description of the way they wanted to be, a description of their ideal self. The ideal was to be attainable rather than some picture of perfection. After a thorough discussion of their ideal, Kelly asked them to play that role for several weeks. He cautioned that they would not likely see much of a result for a while, because it would take at least a couple of weeks for other people to change their reactions to befit the "new" people. At the end of three weeks (or longer) Kelly discussed the experiences with them. Was it as glorious to be the ideal as they had thought it might be? They then evaluated the new behaviors to see which ones, if any, to keep. Through this role playing, people risked behaving differently than they had for years, and were thus free from the prison of their old self-concept.

No matter what helping techniques we choose to use with people, we must always keep in mind three points. We must rely on God, be flexible, and tailor the approach to the individual. As helpers our strongest assets will probably be patience and a willingness to love and understand people through their trials. We are merely flashlights pointing the way to Jesus, the Healer of the self.

4

WANTED: SELF-CONTROL

How can we help someone with a problem if we have that same problem ourselves?

No one has total self-control. It is a universal problem. We all feel a prick of guilt at one point or another as we look over the following signs of breakdown in self-control:

☐ Overeating

☐ Inadequate exercise

☐ Inefficient time management

☐ Uncontrolled tongue (using profanity, criticizing or lying to protect our egos, to name a few)

☐ Yielding to a favorite temptation (perhaps television, video-games, romance novels, sports) when we should be doing something else

☐ Inadequate personal worship (failure to pray, praise, seek God's will or regularly read Scripture)

☐ Emotional self-indulgence

☐ Pride
☐ Persistent sin

Persistent inability to control ourselves forces us to admit our weakness. It is the thorn in our pride, pricking the overinflated self. Failure awakens our conscience like a determined sheepdog which nips our heels at every wrong turn and drives us toward the Shepherd. The Shepherd wants us to live disciplined lives. But he knows that at times we will wander away. In his mercy he appoints the sheepdog to hound the wayward sheep.

We know in our hearts that we cannot be an adequate ruler of our lives. Awareness of our weakness drives us to our knees in front of Jesus, where we find the King of kings who alone is adequate for the task. Even though our own lives are not perfectly self-controlled, however, we can help others with their self-control. But we won't be experts. We'll be fellow explorers.

Confronted with M&Ms

At times I overeat. Two foods especially tempt me: potato chips and M&Ms. I have been known to trample large objects between me and a pack of opened M&Ms. Sometimes I sigh and think of those halcyon days when I was twenty and could eat any food that pleased my eye yet never gain an ounce. No longer. Just the fumes of a salted potato chip send me scurrying for jogging warm-ups. Then it is off to the track (the roads in our neighborhood) to do penance.

At the age of twenty-five, I asked Kirby, my wife, to buy M&Ms and potato chips for me only at Christmas. I figured that if they are not bought, they cannot be eaten. However, for the determined potato chip junkie there are ways around such controls. So at Christmas I got a month's supply, which kept me busy the next eleven months losing the extra weight. At the age of thirty, I asked Kirby to hide any potato chips or M&Ms she found about the house. It worked marvelously. Out of sight, out of mind. I could go literally half a year without a potato chip—and never miss it! Only periodically, in the dead of a sleepless night, would

I hear the Siren call of the chips, luring me toward the shoals of Pork Out Bay. By the age of thirty-five, I had almost forgotten about M&Ms.

Then one day I described to one of my classes my now-conquered cravings for brightly coated chocolate bits. The next day, preparing to lecture, I removed a piece of paper from the lectern. Lo! What fiendish plot was this? My students, checking out whether my techniques in self-control really worked, had devised a diabolical test of will for their hapless professor, placing a package of M&Ms before his very eyes.

I raised my eyes to the class. One hundred pairs of angelically innocent eyes stared back, watching for the slightest sign of weakness. With as much dignity as I could muster I hurled my body over the M&Ms. "They're probably poisoned," I told myself unconvincingly.

Struggling out of my jacket without uncovering the temptations, I laid it over the lectern, covering the M&Ms in the same deft move. Then, to occupy my attention, I started talking. Fast. Collegiate fingers flew, taking notes throughout a lecture nuclear-powered in frenzy. Class over, I strode triumphantly to the lectern, whipped the coat off the package of M&Ms (knocking them to the floor and inadvertently stepping on them), and proclaimed, "See, I don't need M&Ms. I can quit anytime!"

When the last student had left the classroom, I ate every little mangled crumb. And threw away the empty package, shredded in the ravage of its rape.

Hope for Control

Self-control decisions are forced on us when we must choose between two behaviors mutually incompatible.[1] Either I eat the M&Ms or I do not. The dieter cannot simultaneously eat a piece of cheesecake (450 calories, 4 days of guilt) and not eat the cheesecake. A person trying to stop smoking cannot both have an after-dinner cigarette and also keep a record of not smoking. A compulsive gambler cannot place a bet and stop gambling.

All self-control situations involve two competing actions. Each of these has both long- and short-term consequences. For the dieter, eating the cheesecake has the short-term consequence of pleasure in taste, sight, smell and feeling. The long-term consequence is fat. On the other hand, not eating the cheesecake has the short-term consequence of leaving the dieter a bit hungry and deprived of the pleasure of eating; but the long-term consequence is a healthier body.

Almost always self-control situations ask us to choose between a pleasureful now and a pleasureful later. We'd need no discipline if we could have both! So the problem of self-control comes down to how to delay our pleasure (gratification), and how to substitute one type of pleasure for another.

It is not just the short-term rewards that urge us to yield to temptation. Physical and internal cues also stimulate us to give in. Physical cues are sights, sounds and smells that tempt us. When we lack self-control, we respond automatically to physical cues—without considering the long-term consequences. Internal cues, like thoughts or images, might also compel us to go for the immediate reward. For example, our thoughts might excuse us: "I've already burned up that many calories"; "I feel so depressed; I need to have something in my life that is still fun." Such thoughts act as cues for eating, just as Pavlov's bell cued his dogs.

In my case the sight or smell of chips or M&Ms, or even the knowledge that they're in the house, provides an occasion for self-control. They cue me to search and destroy—through eating! The sights and smells of potato chips are especially strong.

Technically speaking, there are two kinds of self-control: restraint and endurance.[2] Both demand that we opt for the long-term benefit. Most of what we've talked about so far has called for restraint. That is, I must deny myself the potato chip now if I want to be slim in the long term. The second kind of self-control, endurance, is called for when the immediate effect is not merely a denial of pleasure but rather a putting up with discomfort or pain. For example, we must let the dentist drill on our teeth now if we wish to have sound teeth years from now. A more extreme illustration of endurance is the martyr's death. The martyr chooses death because of the reward beyond death.

So a friend has come to us with a self-control problem. We start by helping him or her rethink the situation. First, what are the *consequences* of each choice, short-term and long-term? The immediate rewards of giving in to temptation are no doubt stronger than the long-term rewards of restraint or endurance, or the person wouldn't be having a problem with self-control. Second, help rethink possible responses. Could the two alternative *behaviors* be expanded to include *other options?* For example, the dieter could elect to munch on celery rather than either starve or eat cheesecake. Third, rethink the self-control *situation.* Is there a way to change it to make self-control easier? It is always easier to restrain myself from M&Ms when they aren't around. (Help your friend: eat the cheesecake!)

When the Issue Is Sin

We might never think of discussing our friend's eating habits, time-management troubles or critical tongue without being asked. But is it the same when our friend habitually sins? What do we do when our friend engages in persistent sin and we know about it?

We may learn about it inadvertently. A friend seeks help from you for one thing—say, career troubles—but as you talk, you find that sin is incorporated into his or her lifestyle. For example, a woman trying to decide which of two jobs to take mentions in passing that she and her fiancé are living together.

Less common, we may learn about it when a person confides directly to you that she is having problems with some sinful behavior that she can't stop doing. Perhaps a man has become convinced that smoking (or drinking or overeating or any number of self-indulgences) is wrong for him. Whether you agree that the behavior is wrong in principle, you know that the behavior is truly sinful for that person, "for whatever does not proceed from faith is sin" (Rom 14:23).

Why do people indulge in persistent sin? The answer is simple. The remedy is not. People persistently sin because of willful rebellion against God and because the principle of sin is stronger than anyone's will to live the righteous life (see Rom 7). Sin is powerful. And our natural tendency to justify, deny, ignore or cover up sin makes it more difficult to deal with. How quickly our feet run to do evil. How quickly our hearts justify our sin.

Persistent sin is a problem in self-control, and we can help by using the same principles used with any other self-control problem. But first either we must be asked to help or we must confront the problem unbidden. That, in itself, can be problematic.

To Confront or Not to Confront

Should we broach the topic of sin when the friend has not asked for help with it, though he has asked help for something else? That is the first decision to make. If we do decide to discuss it, the second decision is how.

As an elder in a church for a number of years, I saw several instances of church discipline—correcting a Christian who was engaged in persistent public sin. Feelings run high at these times, and opinions of how to rightly divide the Word of God are as numerous as the people involved. Decisions are complicated by unexamined, unconscious and complex motives. Usually we know the person whose sin has become public. Often the person is a friend. Some people are upset when a person in the church is sinning so publicly and the elders say nothing about it. Others are upset if the elders do say something about it. When people in the body of Christ fall into sin, the entire body suffers. If no one approaches them about the sin, they sometimes "self-destruct." They become overridden with anger, bitterness and resentment, and ultimately they fall away from the fellowship. Persistent sin is truly a harbinger of death and destruction.

Biblical arguments can be found on both sides of the issue, to confront or not to confront. One side might quote, "How can you say to your brother, 'Let me take the speck out of your eye,' when there is the log in your own eye? You hypocrite, first take the log out of your own eye, and then you will see clearly to take the speck out of your brother's eye" (Mt 7:4-5). Who can dare stand in the presence of Jesus and claim not to have a logjam in their eyes? Yet the biblical injunction is plain: "If a man is overtaken in any trespass, you who are spiritual should restore him in a spirit of gentleness" (Gal 6:1). Clearly, *some* are called to correct the one who strays.

How can we know whether *we* are to look solely to our own eye, or to look to our brother's? This decision must rest on the Holy Spirit. The Holy Spirit works in a clear enough way. First, if we are tempted to correct another, we must thoroughly examine our motives in the light of the Holy Spirit. Our initial assumption should be that we are *not* to correct our brother or sister. Only if we pray carefully, asking the Lord to reveal our true motives, should we listen to the voice that prompts us to restore our friend. What should that motive be? In the purest form, we must care deeply for the person. The guidance in Galatians is couched in the context that care for the other is paramount. We are to bear one another's burdens and love our friend as ourselves (6:2). We are not to think too highly of ourselves (v. 3). We are to test our own work (v. 4). Only after careful self-examination—more than a cursory overview—praying in the presence of the Holy Spirit, can we see well enough to even attempt to remove the painful splinter from the eye of a friend. It is never hasty.

Ask yourself these questions: Do I really care for the other person? Am I a close enough friend that I am willing to bear his or her burdens? Is the timing right for a confrontation? Is the Holy Spirit directing? If the answer to all these is yes, then consider how to broach the topic of sin. The key is that we restore people "in a spirit of gentleness," lest we too be tempted (Gal 6:1). We might be tempted to judge the person. This is our greatest danger.

Confronting in gentleness, or "speaking the truth in love" (Eph 4:15), means different things to different people. For some, this means merely believing that the person "needs to hear the truth for his own (ultimate) good." A person armed with this conviction often pays little attention to *how* the confrontation proceeds or even to the consequences of the confrontation. Once this person has "spoken the truth" as he or she sees it, the person righteously condemns any behavior that shows less than total and complete compliance. Fortunately, confrontations such as these seldom happen, for most helpers do deeply care about the other person.

A Time for Gentleness

A gentle confrontation begins with the attitude that sin is ultimately harmful. If people continue in sin, they will reap pain, not only in their final judgment (Lk 12:48; 1 Cor 3:10-15) but also in their life on earth (Gal 6:7-10). We might well believe that sin is absolutely wrong, and we might yearn for purity in the church, but we're generally not going to move people toward love and harmony by telling them to get on the path of purity. That kind of confrontation is simply a judgment. That is why Paul admonishes those who confront to "look to yourself, lest you too be tempted" (Gal 6:1). We will accomplish more by expressing tender concern to help people out of their present pain and to help them avoid future pain.

We will also accomplish more if we set a modest goal for the confrontation. Granted, we want people to renounce sin, repent and turn to righteous living. But we can't make that the goal. We would end up pushing people too hard, which provokes them to resist change rather than adopt it. The harder we force people to give up sin, the more we empower the sin nature within them. It is paradoxical. While trying to help people get closer to God, we push them closer to Satan. This happens when we want to accomplish something ourselves instead of being content to let the Holy Spirit convict people to change. We need, rather, to express our love for the person, our concern over the pain we see them about to inflict on themselves (as a result of stepping outside God's guidelines as given in the Scriptures), and our willingness to help them overcome the difficulties in changing. Then we let the Holy Spirit persuade.

The issue is simpler when friends ask for help in dealing with persistent sin in their lives. In this case we can treat the problem just as we would treat any other problem of self-control. In dealing with sin, however, we might experience some feelings not present with a self-control problem like weight or procrastination. First, we will repeatedly have to confront our own vulnerability to sin and our own inability to defeat the old sinful nature. Although Jesus is the key to self-control and we are in Jesus, yet we never arrive at sinless perfection. As John says, "If we say we have no sin, we deceive ourselves, and the truth is not in us" (1 Jn 1:8). This awareness of our vulnerability, which we often struggle to forget, can create a bevy of emotions in us—shame, embarrassment, guilt, self-righteousness, anger and defensiveness. Unaware of these emotions, we might not help our friend. Better to recognize our own sinfulness and deal with it directly with God, getting it out of the way of our relationship with people who are asking for help. Then we can help them fight their sinful behavior.

5

WINNING THE BATTLE FOR SELF-CONTROL

Sad eyes. That was her distinctive feature. At twenty-nine, single and underemployed, Nan gazed through large lenses with sad brown eyes. Her blond hair was slightly ruffled from the March wind, but Martha, Nan's only friend, knew it would look ruffled even in the calm of July. Nan's outfit did not quite fit together, as if it were just too much effort for her to take care of herself—an impression fortified by those brown, basset-hound eyes.

Sitting in her apartment with Martha, Nan lamented her life. It was in general disarray. She had a history of parental rejection and a correspondingly poor self-image. She was chronically in debt. Lonely and deficient in many social skills, Nan had a way of simply staring until silences stretched into minutes. At last she spoke.

"It's discouraging," she said. "I keep failing. I had a date last night, and I ended up getting drunk and going to bed with him. It always ends that way."

"Always?" Martha asked.

"At least once or twice a month, and more often when I'm going out with someone regularly. I can't say no to a guy, especially if he's the least bit aggressive. Oh, I can say no, but they seem to know I don't mean it, and if they keep pushing I'll give in. The drinking—that's just part of the pattern." After a pause, she looked up and said, "I've got to do something about this."

Nan has some serious problems in self-control, maybe too serious for Martha to help with. That's one thing Martha will need to decide. But Nan is reaching out for help. What can Martha do?

If Martha decides she should try to help, the first thing she will do is to encourage Nan to rethink her problem, as we discussed in the last chapter. Now Martha is ready to create an action plan that will help Nan break out of her trap.

Basically Nan has three ways she can tackle her problem— through *consequences, actions* or *situations*. Anyone can be the entrance to growth-producing freedom for her. Martha's role will be to help Nan plan her action. Nan can (1) change the consequences of her decision, (2) change her actions or (3) change the situations that get her into trouble. We'll look at each strategy in general and then see how Martha eventually helped Nan plan her way to self-control.

Changing the Consequences

Option one is to change the consequences of our actions. For instance, we can add rewards, both in the short run and in the long run, for acting with self-control. Or we can add punishment, both in the short and long run, for failure to exert self-control.

Mary, a student in one of my classes, wanted to be more faithful in her morning quiet time. She studied her morning routine and found that, once she picked up her Bible, she was able to have a good devotional time. But too often the short-term pleasure of sleeping in won the day. Mary needed a new cover for her Bible. Pricing them at a local Christian bookstore, she found three covers that were satisfactory: a very nice one for $13, a moderately nice one for $9, and a functional one for $6. Mary could afford the nicest and ordinarily would have bought it outright. However, because she wanted to motivate herself to more frequent quiet times, she devised a plan.

At the beginning of the semester, Mary gave $15 to her room-mate, Suzanne. Every time Mary slept in rather than have devotions, Suzanne was to take 15¢ of the money and spend it however she chose. At the end of the semester, fifteen weeks later, Mary would get back any money still left and use it to buy the new Bible cover.

The plan worked for several reasons. For one, Mary wanted the Bible cover and was willing to work to get it. Since she ordinarily would have bought the cover outright, she was not expanding her budget or bribing herself, but was using a normal part of her life to create incentive and to remind herself daily to have devotions. Second, the plan worked because Mary involved Suzanne, making herself accountable to someone else. This made it more difficult for Mary to forget and then simply excuse herself. Third, this plan worked because it took into account Mary's tendency to fail.

Let's be honest. It is *hard* to break old habits, and it is *unreasonable* to demand perfection from ourselves when we are trying to form new ones. Yet this is often what people do. They begin with such high standards that they cannot hope to succeed for long. Then, when they fail, as they inevitably do, they say, "Heaven knows I tried. I did my best. But I just can't control myself." This cycle perpetuates problems in self-control and promotes discouragement.

Another way to use consequences to increase self-control is to make the long-term results more immediate. Louise wanted to improve her study habits. Besides feeling bad when she got low grades, Louise knew that her mother would give her a real "chewing out," with her "voice like a buzz saw and language so fierce it makes paint peel from the walls." Though she knew what to expect from her mother, Louise had not been able to exert enough self-control during the previous semester to keep her grades as high as they had been during her freshman year.

Here's what she did. Louise visited her mother during the second week of the semester, when "the wounds were still raw from the Christmas grade report period." Louise remarked casually, "I think I'm probably going to party a lot this semester; these courses don't look any harder than the ones I took last semester." Suddenly there was a spark of electricity in the air, and the buzz saw was grinding away. "Why, she chewed me up one side and down the other and all around the corners too. When she finished with me, my ego was so ground up it felt like raw hamburger. But you know, that chewing out really helped me," Louise confided. "Not the way Mama thought. You see, I had my tape recorder running, and I taped Mom's whole discourse on my study habits. Now, each night after dinner at school, I go back to my room and turn on the tape. After listening for a minute or two, I run, not walk, to the books. Why, once when Sam asked me to go out for a pizza on the night before a big test, I had to listen to the whole tape twice before I turned him down. But I made a B on that test!"

Changing Our Actions

Most people think of self-control as an all-or-nothing proposition. Either we are self-controlled or we are not. There is no middle ground. This is *not* a good way to think about the problem. No one is perfect. At times we all fail to exercise control. Thinking in all-or-nothing terms can discourage us from going on with self-discipline. Problem drinkers, for example, will periodically quit drinking. They may exert great effort to resist taking a drink—and succeed for months. But if one sip occurs, it often means weeks of drinking, accompanied by self-blame and guilt. Some time later they again quit drinking, and the cycle repeats.

Better than the all-or-nothing approach to self-control is knowing that we might be self-controlled in some areas but not others. One person might manage her time very efficiently but be unable to control eating. Another might have remarkable self-discipline in physical matters—not smoking, not overeating, exercising regularly—but find television addicting, spending hours watching the soaps or sitcoms. Some may even be addicted—perish the thought—to potato chips or M&Ms. Still, even this is not the best way to think of self-control.

It is best to view control as making a series of decisions. Each decision is new. In a sense it has no history. Twenty years of successful self-control do not guarantee that the next decision will be one that shows discipline. The people of Alcoholics Anonymous understand this principle. They insist that a person with a drinking problem acknowledge himself or herself as an incurable alcoholic. This establishes the mindset that to slip on self-control is always possible, but it does not mean that we will necessarily slip the next time. Each decision stands alone.

In this sense a person can live a self-controlled life daily without ever becoming self-controlled. For those seeking a simple answer to the problem of aligning their human will with God's, this may be discouraging. The fact is, though, that God does not align our will with his permanently. Not only would this destroy meaningful life by eliminating our decision making, but it would also destroy our reliance on God. God wants us to choose him continually. We will never be totally God-controlled. Nor will we ever become totally self-controlled. But with God's help we can choose self-control almost continually throughout our lives, even though we occasionally will fail.

When we understand that each situation calling for self-control is a cue for choosing God, we are freed to think creatively about how we might overcome the temptation we are experiencing. We are not locked into the same behaviors day after day. We are free to ask ourselves, "How can I meet this new challenge in a way that will glorify God?"

And we can help others do the same. We can help them be creative in controlling themselves. For example, draw on your own experiences. How have you dealt with strong temptations? Disclose these instances and suggest that they might work for others. Caution them that what worked for you might not work for them. Try to promote an attitude of experimentation. We want them to test many ideas to find what works for them.

Help them think about how they will handle decision points, times when they are forced to either fall to temptation or choose an alternate behavior. Can they anticipate when they will likely have to make the next decision? If so, talk them through that instance, showing alternative ways the temptation can be dealt with.

As Dennis and I were talking one day, the topic turned to our marriages. Dennis had been married to Sharon for six years. A strong Christian man, he worked as assistant manager at a local country club. Sharon worked as a model for local and regional clothing companies and often traveled during the week. Still in their mid-twenties, they had no children.

Dennis: Ev, can I ask you a personal question?

Me: Sure.

Dennis: Do you have fantasies about other women besides Kirby? I mean, well, I've been having trouble lately keeping my thoughts in line.

Me: How so?

Dennis: Well, I love Sharon and we have a good relationship in all areas. I mean we have a good sex life and everything. But I find myself watching some of the women around the pool at the club and having vivid sexual fantasies. I could understand it if I weren't satisfied with Sharon, but it doesn't make sense to me the way it is.

Me: Sounds like you're worried about it. Is it just one particular woman that you think about?

Dennis: No. (Pause) I think about several, but one more than others, I guess. I even think about some of the high-school girls. That's kind of sick. I wouldn't act on it, of course, but I get frustrated knowing it really isn't good to be imagining such things and not being able to stop.

Me: You seem bothered by a number of things. One, you can't control your thoughts and you think you should. Two, you fantasize too much about one particular woman. Three, you fantasize about high-school girls. And four, it bothers you that you fantasize at all when your sexual relationship with Sharon is good.

Dennis: You got it, but some of the problems are worse than others. I really don't have that much problem thinking about the teen-agers. I cut those fantasies off pretty quick. It's more not being able to stop thinking about Marjorie. That's the worst. Once I start thinking about her, I usually have a full-blown love affair in my mind. I know I shouldn't, so don't tell me that. But how to stop it—that's what I don't know.

Me: You seem to really want to stop, but just don't know how. (He nods.) What usually starts the fantasies?

Dennis: Just seeing her at the pool. She's about thirty-three and has taken very good care of her body. She has blond hair and smooth skin, very tan, and I start off thinking about putting suntan lotion on her. Then it's off to the races.

Me: Are there other times that you have these fantasies?

Dennis: Not really. It is pretty much always the same. Not much variety in my fantasy life, I guess.

Me: You've tried a number of ways to stop the fantasies?

Dennis: Some. Usually I just think, "I've got to stop this and get back to work."

Me: How does that work?

Dennis: It works about one out of four or five times, maybe. Usually though, I just stare at my papers and go on with the fantasy. I don't really abandon myself to it, but I just can't stop it.

Me: You've tried other ways?

Dennis: Yeah. I scold myself. I tell myself that I shouldn't be thinking those things and that God disapproves and that it is certainly not edifying and not good for my marriage. All those things don't work worth beans. If I catch myself early before I get into the fantasy, sometimes it turns me off, but I usually don't catch myself that early.

Me: What other ways have you tried?

Dennis: I can't think of others right now.

Me: How do you stop thinking about the teen girls when you get started in that direction?

Dennis: Well, I usually don't get started much in that direction. I just think, "This is crazy. It's just a fantasy, 'cause she's just a kid." That usually turns off the fantasy right away.

Me: What do you suppose would happen if you told yourself the same thing when you started thinking about Mary, or what did you say her name . . . ?

Dennis: Marjorie. Well, it wouldn't work, I don't think. You see, it somehow doesn't seem like quite as much of a fantasy with her. It should, I guess. Good grief, she has a teen-age daughter herself. She's divorced. I never thought about it much before.

Me: From what you say, Dennis, she doesn't sound exactly like your type.

Dennis: Yeah, I know that, but . . . I was going to say that I never really thought about it as a long-term relationship with her. That would be absurd. I don't think I could do any better than Sharon. I mean, she's better all around. Prettier, too. And really sexier when you come right down to it.

Me: Do you ever have fantasies about Sharon?

Dennis: (Laughs) That's a good question! Funny thing is, I used to—really steamy ones too. But I haven't really thought much about it in several years.

Me: It just seemed to me that if you had a fantasy about Sharon whenever you started to think about Marjorie, it might stop you from having the fantasy about her.

Dennis: That makes a lot of sense.

Me: How are you going to do it? Let's say you are working at your club and you look out the window and see Marjorie at the pool. What are you going to think to yourself that reminds you of your strategy?

Dennis: Well, if I start to think along those lines—and I don't always go off on a fantasy at the drop of a hat—but if I start, I'll just try to switch my thinking to the old fantasy I used to have of Sharon modeling bathing suits for me.

Me: You think that will do it? Will it get your fantasy changed?

Dennis: I don't really know, but I think it's got the best chance of anything I've tried so far. We'll see!

Me: Do you think that fantasy of Sharon will get old and not be able to hold your attention after a while?

Dennis: No. I had it continually for about three years. I don't know exactly why I stopped thinking about it. I told you that my fantasy life doesn't show much variety.

Talking with Dennis the next summer, I asked him about his struggle with fantasy. He said he had tried to use the fantasy of Sharon to regularly avert his fantasy about Marjorie and found it worked about seventy-five percent of the time. Then he had decided to spice up some of his fantasies about Sharon by initiating some new behaviors into their love-making routine. Now both he and Sharon thought their sexual relationship was better than ever. Thus far this summer, he said, he had rarely been troubled by fantasies of other women.

This conversation illustrates one way of helping a person realize that he must make self-controlling decisions at every temptation point. It also shows how to help the person explore and choose a new way of acting over the old pattern he's tempted to follow. Finally, it illustrates how to help the person figure out how he is going to use the chosen behavior in the tempting situation.

Changing the Situation

Your friend is about to step into a tempting situation. At this point he still has two ways out. First, he may enter the situation and then work to change it. Second, he can anticipate the situation and simply avoid it altogether or change it before it begins to tempt. Avoiding temptation altogether is generally the easiest way out because it requires only one decision—and that made while not in the presence of the tempting cues!

Recall the strategies I used to control my weakness for potato chips and M&Ms. First I worked on changing the situation so that I could avoid the temptation. We bought no (or few) chips. When we did buy them, Kirby hid them from me. (In our house that merely meant putting them out of sight in a cupboard. I even knew where they were hidden, but it worked anyway because the chips were out of sight.) When students gave me the package of M&Ms, I tried the same strategy even though I was already in the tempting situation: I covered the M&Ms with my coat. Lastly, I changed the internal cues that prompted me to eat; that is, I changed my thinking. First I thought (unconvincingly) that the M&Ms were poisoned and then I used the situation (my lecture) to occupy my thoughts. All these strategies can be used in helping a friend who needs to change the situation—by leaving it or changing physical or internal cues.

The Bible has a lot to say about temptations. Scripture recommends dealing with it by avoiding the situation or leaving it. In *The Fight* (IVP, 1976) John White paints a memorable picture.[1] Imagine this scene: Satan is standing behind us, just off our right shoulder, whispering in our ear. "Go on," he says with sibilant smoothness. "Do it. Just one time won't matter. God will forgive you. Just bite the apple. It'll taste good. It's beautiful. God made it for your enjoyment. It'll make you wise—even more spiritual than you are now. Won't Adam be proud of you?" As he whispers, he spreads the temptation before our eyes regaling us with the "lust of the flesh and the lust of the eyes and the pride of life" (1 Jn 2:16). We enjoy the sensations of the temptation, then slowly reach out our hand.

But Scripture admonishes us to turn from temptation. Literally we are to remove the temptation from our sight. Speaking of the temptation to adultery, Jesus says, "But I say to you that every one who looks at a woman lustfully has already committed adultery with her in his heart. If your right eye causes you to sin, pluck it out and throw it away. . . . If your right hand causes you to sin, cut it off and throw it away" (Mt 5:28-30). A paraphrase: If you might sin through looking, don't look; if you might sin through touching, don't touch.

When we turn away from sin and temptation, however, we come face to face with the tempter. But Scripture tells us how to deal with him. "Resist the devil and he will flee from you" (Jas 4:7). "No temptation has overtaken you that is not common to man. God is faithful, and he will not let you be tempted beyond your strength, but with the temptation will also provide the way of escape, that you may be able to endure it" (1 Cor 10:13). Physical avoidance of temptation is not cowardly. It is God's way of making self-control easier.

Changing the physical cues involves arranging, before the time of temptation, cues that promote self-control. Diane, twenty-five pounds overweight, was irresistibly drawn to the refrigerator. She decided to set up some physical cues at her point of temptation, namely, the refrigerator. First, she took out the lightbulb so it would be more difficult to see inside. Second, she bought several opaque containers, keeping her from easily seeing what foods were stored. Third, she bought twenty-five pounds of pork fat from the butcher, which she hung in a cellophane bag in the front of the refrigerator door. Each time she lost a pound, she removed a pound of pork fat from the bag and threw it away. If she gained a pound, she had to go back to the butcher and add a pound of fat to the bag. She had made her place of temptation a reminder of self-control through physical cues.

Perhaps the most natural way of controlling ourselves in tempting situations is to divert our attention to something else.[2] Psychologist Walter Mischel tested children to find out how they coped with temptation. First, he gave each child a choice between two fresh marshmallows and a small pretzel. Almost all the children chose the marshmallows. Mischel then explained he was going to leave the room. The children could eat the pretzel any time they wanted, or if they could wait for Mischel's return without eating the pretzel, then they could have the marshmallows instead. The children had to wait sitting in a chair directly in front of the pretzel, prominently visible as a constant temptation. Mischel left the room and watched the children's behavior through a one-way mirror.

Children successful at controlling their desire for fifteen minutes used a variety of self-distracting strategies. Some looked away or covered their eyes with their hands. Others sang—louder as the temptation got stronger. Some played with toys or their hands. One even went to sleep. Children who were unsuccessful at self-control stared at the pretzel, thought about it, and described aloud how hungry they were and how good the pretzel or marshmallows would taste.

Adults too can use mental diversion to distract themselves from temptation. They can recognize that self-control is not merely a battle of the flesh but is also part of the spiritual warfare we are all engaged in. They can pray for strength and for God to reveal the way out of the temptation (see 1 Cor 10:13). They can be alert for God's answer, how he will help them conquer temptation in this particular case. Finally, they can change their internal thoughts and images to distract themselves from the temptation.

Nan and Martha

Nan had asked for help with her promiscuity and drinking. Martha wants to help but needs to find out more. Since she can learn more by asking about a particular instance than by talking about the problem in general terms, Martha asks Nan about what happened the night before.

"What is the pattern? For example, exactly what happened

when you were out on that date last night?"

Nan spoke. "He took me out to a nice restaurant. We had a bottle of wine with dinner, and we went back to his apartment to watch television. We had a couple of drinks, and he suggested it, and I couldn't say no. So we did it."

"And that's the pattern, huh?"

"Yeah, always different, but alike too. I don't even drink except on dates."

"What goes on in your head? What do you think about when he's trying to get you to have sex and you're trying to refuse?"

"I guess I think, 'I shouldn't. It's not right. He really doesn't care for me.' Things like that. And I think about how I know it's pointless to say no because I know it will probably end in bed anyway. I know I'm weak. This kind of stuff has been going on since I was in high school. Besides, I like it." Haltingly, Nan continued, "I have this battle with myself, an argument in my mind. I try to deny that I like to make love but it doesn't do any good. It does feel good. I like the security of having a man close, even if I know it's just for the night and even if I know that I'll probably never see him again."

"So that's half of the argument: It feels good. What's the other half?"

"Well, the other half is my Christian upbringing. I know it is a sin. I know it angers God. I even know that he probably won't forgive me because I do it so willingly. It makes it hard to live with. It's my body battling my mind, and body is winning."

"Sounds like you've thought through it and have decided to let your body win."

"No," Nan objected. "I've tried everything. I've had prayers for deliverance. I've had prayers for strength. I've had prayers for healing. I always go away resolved never to let it happen again. It usually lasts until my first or maybe second date, if I'm lucky. I just don't have the will power to say no."

"Do you want to be able to say no?"

"Of course I do! Do you think I _like_ to live like this?"

"Well, I believe that if you have prayed for deliverance and healing and strength, then God has surely answered or is answering. What we need to do is find a way that the answer can show up in your life, and that means devising a plan for you to say no when your mind tells you you should resist."

"You mean learning how to turn a guy off whenever I want?" asked Nan.

"I mean sometimes God takes away your desire to sin. But sometimes he wants you to choose to obey, even if it is hard. We know that the Bible says that you won't have any temptation that others don't have too, and that God is faithful and won't let you be tested beyond your power to resist. He will provide a way out. We need to find the way out that he is providing *for you*. Obviously, until now you haven't found the way that he has provided. Let's experiment and find out what does work."

Over the next fifteen minutes, Nan and Martha identify what the tempting situations have in common. Drinking is one obvious similarity. Talk then turns to Nan's "point of no return" in her sexual encounters, which is the point after which she hardly ever chooses to stop.

Martha then said, "We need to look at how to change the situation to make it easier to say no."

"The only easy way to say no is to never have a date again, and I'm not ready to go that far."

"That's definitely the idea though," said Martha. "If you arrange things far enough in advance, before you get to that point of no return, you stand a better chance of making a decision you'll be happier with in the morning. You have to interrupt the normal chain of events somewhere, maybe at several points."

"I guess I could not drink wine with the meal or no drinks with the guy afterward. I guess it wouldn't be that hard not to drink on a date. I never drink any other time so it's not like I am addicted or anything."

"Is there any other way you might break the normal chain of events?"

"I guess we could go back to my apartment instead of his. The problem is that it is just a very long time from the beginning of a date until the end of an evening. We can talk some of the time, but I can't honestly see myself, a thirty-year-old woman, sitting around chatting like a schoolgirl for hours. I don't think there is anything wrong with me for wanting to be close to a guy or do some heavy making out. I don't want to cut all of that out."

"Is there any way that you could change the expectations of the men you date before it gets to the point of their initiating sex?" asked Martha.

"I guess I could discuss it with them ahead of time, but I've never been very good at that. I could try. It has worked in the past when I've done it. I just haven't done it in a while. Hey, I've got some pretty good plans here! I'm anxious to try some of these ideas out. I think they might work."

A Time for Compassion

Nothing fires the righteous indignation quite as much as seeing people who can't control themselves in an area where we can. If overeating is not a problem for us, we often feel superior to those who overeat. If we do not drink, the alcoholic seems weak to us. If we keep tight rein on our emotions, we can easily despise those whose emotions are in the driver's seat.

Yet, if we are sensitive, other people's struggles can move us to a deeper understanding of our own weaknesses and to a genuine compassion for them. We must be vigilant as helpers not to judge people who have a problem we do not have. In Galatians 6:1-3 Paul says, "Brethren, if a man is overtaken in any trespass, you who are spiritual should restore him in a spirit of gentleness. Look to yourself, lest you too be tempted. Bear one another's burdens, and so fulfil the law of Christ. For if any one thinks he is something, when he is nothing, he deceives himself."

We must not place a guilt trip on people who succumb to temptation. It is easy to become frustrated when we try to help and yet they continue to fail. The natural response is to retaliate either with overt anger, criticism or accusation, or with covert anger such as guilt making, sarcasm or gossip.

What should we do when they fail? First, treat failure as a chance to ask why they failed and then to see what they can do about those causes. Do not condemn. Before offering suggestions for action, explore together (1) why the person wants to change, (2) what the consequences for failing to change are, and (3) how the person has already tried to solve the problem. Remember that many (perhaps most) people, when they ask for your help, want your support. They are less interested in your suggestions than in knowing you care about them. Not that we shouldn't offer suggestions, but we should realize the need for careful, respectful, caring listening as the basis of helping. Only when we know what a person has to bear can we help bear his burdens.

Above all, recognize that God will always provide a way out of temptation for those who sincerely seek him. If we can help people increase their enthusiasm for knowing the Lord, then most of the battle is won. The techniques we've talked about here are merely useful to "mop up" after the main victory.

6

THE TYRANNY
OF FEAR

She sat in my office and shook all over. "I've always been this way," she groaned. "But lately it has gotten so bad that I can't even think about failing."

Nancy was a college student who had come to me for counseling because she was afraid—literally petrified—of failing. She worried about school, about her part-time job, about disappointing her parents and, although she was only eighteen, about being an "old maid." Her fear was paralyzing her. She said she could do nothing all day long except stay in her room and think. She smoked five cigarettes during our one-hour interview. It was clear to me that Nancy was deep in the clutches of anxiety. What had caused her to become so anxious? What could be done to help her conquer her fears?

As we consider helping the anxious person, we will first look at why people become so anxious and fearful. Then we will outline an overall helping strategy based on that understanding.

Sigmund Freud saw a difference between fear and anxiety. Fear occurs when we have some "objective" reason to believe that we may be hurt. Anxiety, on the other hand, is a result of unconscious conflicts; for example, we may fear being overcome by some uncontrollable impulse. Like many other modern psychologists, however, I do not find it helpful to make such a distinction between anxiety and fear.[1] I prefer to treat fear and anxiety as both involving the same mental process—anticipation of harm.

Fear began in the Garden of Eden. Adam and Eve had acted in a way that glorified themselves rather than God. They knew the consequences of their behavior—death. As they waited for God in the garden, they tried to hide from him. As God approached, he called out, "Where are you?" Amazing. The Creator and Lord of the entire universe is asking two people within a garden where they were. Surely God's question involved more than finding the physical location of Adam and Eve.

Adam answered God, "I heard the sound of thee in the garden, and I was afraid, because I was naked; and I hid myself" (Gen 3:10). Anticipating the worst, Adam was afraid. And he had good reason to be afraid. Because of his action he was cut off from God's presence.

The fear of ultimate separation from God has permeated the human race since the time of Adam. Yet God has, through Jesus' death, re-established contact with all humans who will have it. In his letter to the Romans, Paul tells us that we are faced with the same choice today that Adam had so long ago:

So then, brethren, we are debtors, not to the flesh, to live according to the flesh—for if you live according to the flesh you will die, but if by the Spirit you put to death the deeds of the body you will live. For all who are led by the Spirit of God are sons of God. For you did not receive the spirit of slavery to fall back into fear, but you have received the spirit of sonship. When we cry, "Abba! Father!" it is the Spirit himself bearing witness with our spirit that we are children of God, and if children, then heirs, heirs of God and fellow heirs with Christ, provided we suffer with him in order that we may also be glorified with him. I consider that the sufferings of the present time are not worth comparing with the glory that is to be revealed to us. (Rom 8:12-18)

Paul is claiming that Christians need no longer fear God's judgment. Instead of the awful consequences we deserve, we will experience the wonderful results of Jesus' sacrifice.

John echoes what Paul said: "So we know and believe the love God has for us. God is love, and he who abides in love abides in God, and God abides in him. In this is love perfected with us, that we may have confidence for the day of judgment, because as he is so are we in this world. There is no fear in love, but perfect love casts out fear. For fear has to do with punishment, and he who fears is not perfected in love" (1 Jn 4:16-18).

So fear is the belief that we will experience something awful. While Christians need not fear a disastrous eternity, however, we may well experience fear about things in ordinary life. This is not bad, or unchristian. God created us with the ability to anticipate consequences just so that we could be safe. If we can anticipate harm, we can avoid it. But sometimes people, even Christians, are *too* fearful, and their fear interferes with their lives. Something has gone wrong.

The Feeling of Fear

Fear usually begins as an emotional experience. It may happen in actuality or within our imagination, but either way it is called a *trauma*.[2]

In a trauma our bodies get very busy. Adrenaline is pumped into our blood stream, creating a jittery feeling. Our stomachs might become queasy, our chests tight, our breathing irregular, our face flushed, our mouth dry, our palms clammy and our fingers shaky. This bodily reaction comes from our *sympathetic nervous system* (SNS) getting ready for "fight-or-flight." It is ready to defend us or help us run from harm. At this point we appraise the situation to see how we should label our arousal. As far as our

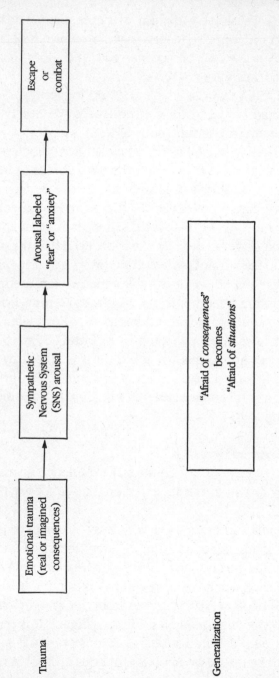

Figure 1. From Trauma to Generalization

body is concerned, it doesn't care whether we feel anger, fear, surprise, sadness or even happiness. But what emotion we *say* we have determines specifically what emotion we will feel. Finally, we escape from the situation or combat it to prevent the feared consequence from occurring. How much lasting impact the trauma has on us depends on how much emotion we felt during it.

The lasting impact is what we generalize from our experience of trauma. Instead of saying, "I am afraid of falling off a mountain and killing myself," I begin to say, "I am afraid of high places." Notice the shift: no longer am I afraid of anticipated consequences; now I am afraid of *all* situations like the one I felt fear in. This generalization is both natural and useful, because it allows us to avoid situations that might be harmful, but it can breed unnecessary fears (see figure 1). Our fears can grow, perpetuating themselves and shriveling our lives as we avoid more and more.

Suppose that some time has passed since the trauma. It was last summer that David fell off the pony at boys' camp. David's fear of falling from the pony has generalized to a fear of all horses. Now his mom offers him another chance at camp this year. This cue (camp) is enough to set off anxiety about horses and all that can go wrong. David isn't so sure he wants to go, though he doesn't know why. When people worry, they imagine—again and again—situations that they think might have terrible consequences. And they feel again those physical symptoms of fear—trembling, sweating and the other flight-or-fight reactions.

When adults observe their bodies showing fear, they sometimes think how afraid or anxious they are. Then they begin to worry about controlling their fears. They become afraid of being afraid. This arouses them even more. Now they try harder to avoid cues (events, places) for anxiety, which makes it even more difficult to rid themselves of their fear. So the cycle of trauma leading to fear and then to worry feeds itself, leaving the victim miserable and feeling hopeless of ever getting out (see figure 2).

Nancy came to me for counseling because of her fear of failure. Her trauma was not a single incident but rather a childhood of

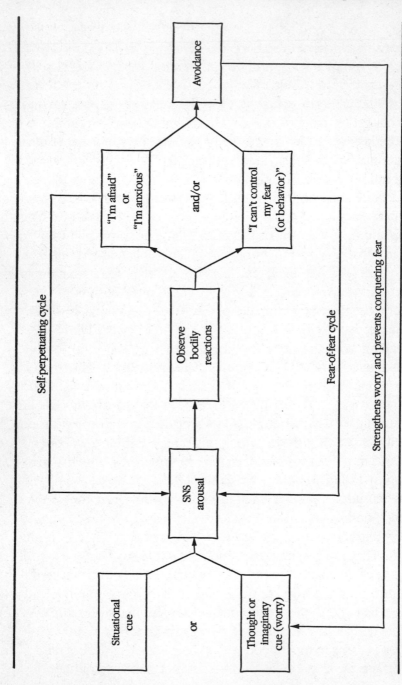

Figure 2. The Fear-Worry Cycle

living with a demanding mother. An only child, Nancy was pushed into activities that her mother had done successfully as a girl. She joined the school band at her mother's insistence, but quit in high school when she found that she could not excel. She ran for student government and went out for cheerleader, losing both competitions. Each time there were emotional scenes at home. Although Nancy's mother did not scold her, she over-reacted emotionally. She became more sad about Nancy's failures than Nancy did.

In time, Nancy began to feel that her mother would be disappointed no matter how she performed. The only thing that Nancy excelled at during high school was academic performance. In college she came to believe that if she were to fail to make all A's her mother would become incurably depressed—and it would be Nancy's fault. Any evaluation was threatening because evaluation implied potential for failure and for disappointing her mother. Nancy's sympathetic nervous system was working over-time. She was upset so frequently that she hated to get out of bed in the mornings. She could not imagine herself succeeding at anything. She even had trouble imagining herself trying to do anything.

Nancy needed extended help. Her anxiety was so severe that she wisely chose professional counsel. As we worked at uncovering some of the reasons for her anxiety and understanding how she perpetuated her fear, she began to venture more. Counseling Nancy was arduous work. We tried many approaches before Nancy finally conquered the tyranny of fear—but she did it.

7

CALMING THE FEARFUL

I was in the Navy during the Vietnam era, but my really harrowing experiences came during training. I'm talking about the swimming test that everyone had to pass.

I don't swim well. In fact, my backstroke looks more like a backhand, and my freestyle looks like . . . well, can you picture a sumo wrestler doing water ballet?

Now, if a trainee failed the swimming test, he had to attend "stupid swim," which meant every afternoon in the pool while everyone else had the only free hour of the day. I was *motivated* to pass the test. We had to swim one hundred yards with our uniform on (any stroke) then jump from a tower into the pool—and survive.

I took off on the one-hundred-yard swim in fine form and clawed my way for about sixty yards. Concentrating on staying alive (I've never been so tired in my life), I swam right between the legs of a guy floating leisurely on his back doing the elementary backstroke and blowing little streams of water through his teeth. I tried to change direction and go around him. I was in deep trouble. Scratching, sputtering and coughing, I fought my way to the end of the pool. I threw my arms over the end of the pool and held on. Everyone else was out of the pool and lined up for the jump from the tower. Through a din of splashing I heard the chief yell, "Don't none uh youse guys help them guys out from the pool." I could have cried.

When I pulled myself from the water, the chief was telling the group how to jump from a burning ship, which the tower was supposed to represent. "Keep your toes pointed downwards," he bawled. "Keep your legs together. Cross your arms and hold onto your nose. Like this." He demonstrated, looking like a pretzel about to leap into hot oil. Give me hot oil any day . . . from a *low* platform.

"Awright, now. Is any uh youse guys afraid to jump off this here little tower?" he asked.

This was my big chance. He wasn't going to make us jump. I struggled to get my hand into the air. Sweat popped out all over my body. My muscles were so tired that I couldn't lift my arm. I tried to lift my right arm with my left hand. I beat on my shoulder. At last I got it started.

"Okay. Youse guys wid your hands up is first," he yelled. "And if youse don't jump, I'm goin' ta throws yuh off!" (Actually, the chief had graduated from Harvard, but he had learned early that you get less cooperation from trainees when you say, "I would like for you to use muscular contractions to propel yourself from the tower gracefully into the water," than when you say, "And if youse don't jump, I'm goin' ta throws yuh off!")

I sprained my wrist getting my arm down before the chief saw it. But finally it was my turn. I stood on the edge of the tower with two other trainees. My legs had betrayed me by climbing the tower of their own volition. I remembered everything that the chief said. I pointed my toes, locked my knees together and held my nose.

Suddenly the air was split with the chief's whistle. I leaped into space. The trip downward seemed to be in slow motion. My life passed before my eyes. Gradually, a piercing scream penetrated my consciousness. Someone was yelling hysterically. I looked down. It was me! My toes were pointed but my legs were spread wide. My arms were waving wildly and my mouth was open. Here came the water.

The fact that I am here today is a testimony to God's saving power. I don't know how else I ever got to the side.

Unhelpful Hints

Our chief got everyone to jump from the tower, but I would consider his methods unconventional at best. He didn't help me overcome my fear. He merely made me more afraid of what would happen if I *didn't* jump than if I *did.* This method is often practiced by parents. It usually goes under the title of "There's Nothing to Be Afraid of in a Dark Room." Every child that has ever been sent into a dark room and told that there's nothing to be afraid of knows that his or her parent is crazy. There are *lots* of things to be afraid of in a dark room—like fear itself for a start. The fear-of-fear cycle makes it difficult for a person to get over fear by facing it and finding no adverse effects. Rather, facing fear head-on has very unpleasant effects. It scares people, and the body sends insistent messages saying, "Never repeat this experience, at all costs." While "plunging right in" is a good way to cope with low levels of fear, it seldom works with high levels.

In fact, common fears can be handled a good many ways. When people become afraid, they try to cope with their fear and generally do so quite creatively. Over the past seven years, I have asked members of my psychology classes how they cope with fear, anxiety or "nervousness." Their answers may be grouped into three broad categories: avoidance, attention diversion and analysis. *Avoidance* includes sleeping, taking drugs or alcohol, and plunging right in without thinking. *Attention diversion* includes things like talking about or thinking about something besides the feared activity, thinking about something pleasurable, and even denying that one is afraid. *Analysis* involves thinking through the situation and the fear: examining the situation objectively (as though it were happening to someone else), collecting information about the probabilities of various outcomes, realizing that the outcome probably will not be catastrophic, thinking about a positive outcome, figuring out how best to cope, and praying.

Most of these common coping techniques do relieve fear. When people ask for help with a fear, however, they have usually tried these techniques and *they have failed.* Something more is needed.

And You Said, "Do Not Fear" (Lam 3:57 NIV)

The best antidote to unhealthy fear is to "fear the Lord." For those who do not believe, the fear of the Lord (that is, fear of the consequences for not being in a right relationship with God) means one thing (Mt 10:28). But Christians don't need to fear those consequences.[1] How then are we to fear him? A study of the Psalms and the Proverbs tells us. God wants us to *praise* him (Ps 22:23); that is, he wants us to tell him that we believe he is doing a good job running the universe. When we praise children, we express our pleasure at what they are doing, and God wants us to agree that his behavior is exemplary. God wants us to *trust* him (Ps 115:11). He wants us to lean on him minute by minute, to put our whole life in his hands. He wants us to *bless* him (Ps 135:20). This means glorifying God for his character. We are to *serve* God (Ps 2:11), knowing that we were created for good works (Eph 2:8-10). We are to *hate evil* (Prov 8:13) and *depart from it* (Prov 3:7). Through this right attitude and right behavior, we show proper fear of the Lord.

This fear does not produce avoidance and paralysis. Rather it wakes us up to our glorious inheritance and his immeasurable power alive in us (Eph 1:18-19). God has demonstrated his mercy and pity (Ps 103:11-12), which lead to our salvation (Ps 85:9) and eternal life (Jn 6:47). God will be with us (Ps 25:14), watching over us (Ps 33:18), and he will provide knowledge, wisdom and instruction (Prov 1:7; 9:10). When we fear the Lord, we experience the opposite of normal fear. Fearing God is reverently trusting him.

When we are tempted to fear, we must choose instead to trust the Lord. We can consciously place ourselves in his care, for he can save us. Several verses tell us to counteract fear, worry or anxiety with trust. Figure 3 contains verses that deal directly with coping with fear.² Read each one slowly and savor it. Picture the images they offer. They are powerful. Psalm 23, which is overflowing with rich imagery, has seen many people through trying times.

High-level Fear

Psalm 23:4 I fear no evil; for thou art with me; thy rod and thy staff, they comfort me.

Psalm 27:1 The LORD is my light and my salvation; whom shall I fear? The LORD is the stronghold of my life; of whom shall I be afraid?

Psalm 46:1-2 God is our refuge and strength, a very present help in trouble. Therefore we will not fear . . .

Psalm 56:3-4 When I am afraid, I put my trust in thee. In God, whose word I praise, in God I trust without a fear. What can flesh do to me?

Psalm 118:6 With the LORD on my side I do not fear. What can man do to me?

Proverbs 29:25 The fear of man lays a snare, but he who trusts in the LORD is safe.

Low-level Fear (Worry and Anxiety)

Matthew 6:25-33 Do not be anxious about your life. . . . If God so clothes the grass of the field, which today is alive and tomorrow is thrown into the oven, will he not much more clothe you, O men of little faith? Therefore do not be anxious. . . . But seek first his kingdom and his righteousness.

Philippians 4:6-7 Have no anxiety about anything, but in everything by prayer and supplication with thanksgiving let your requests be made known to God. And the peace of God, which passes all understanding, will keep your hearts and your minds in Christ Jesus.

1 Peter 5:7 Cast all your anxieties on him [God], for he cares about you.

_____

Figure 3. Biblical Help with Fear

Psychology has recently discovered this principle. Most of the effective treatments of fear and anxiety use vivid imagery. *Systematic desensitization,* a powerful technique, replaces images of people acting in fear with images of people behaving calmly.[3] In *stress inoculation,* another method psychologists use, people imagine themselves becoming afraid and then coping with the fear.[4] Two other techniques, *flooding* and *implosion,* also use imagery to help the fearful person.[5] These two techniques involve imagining the worst possible events and concluding that even these are not to be feared.

We generally experience fear as irrational; that is, we know in our heads we should not be afraid, yet we are. Fear is partly irrational. To conquer irrational fear, we may need to try a nonrational solution. Reprogramming our mental imagery is just that. By the time most people come to therapy, they have tried everything that usually works for low-level fear control. Changing images, though, is less commonly thought of.

When we go to help friends with fear, we are wise to pray that the Lord will give them a vision that can replace the fear-provoking image they habitually see. If the new image replaces the old, they may find themselves free from the tyranny of fear.

Scared Stiff

Laura stayed late after Bible study to talk with Ann, a close friend. Laura, a newly-wed, was having difficulty adjusting to married life. One major problem was that her husband worked a rotating shift at a nearby factory and so was often gone at night.

Laura: What I'm really afraid of is being at home alone at night. Even now, when I think of going back to the house later and not having Al there with me . . . Well, it almost makes me sick.

Ann: I can see it really affects you! You got all white and nervous looking.

Laura: Right. Just look at my hand! (Holds up hand, which is shaking) I'm petrified to think about being in that dark house alone.

Ann: You sound scared stiff—immobilized.

Laura: I am. I'm scared! And the funny thing is that I know i doesn't make any sense to be afraid. It's crazy.

Ann: But the fear sure seems real.

Laura: It sure does!

Ann: How do you feel physically when you become afraid? What does your body do?

Laura: I get all fluttery in the stomach. My face feels hot and my hands start to shake. Sometimes my knees even knock together. I had always heard of knocking knees, but I didn't know it could really happen until I got this fear. It's embarrassing.

Ann: Embarrassing?

Laura: Yeah. You know, I should be able to control this fear . . .

Ann: But . . .

Laura: But, well, I can't.

Ann: That in itself must be frightening.

Laura: Let me tell you, it is!

Ann: Laura, when you go into your house at night and Al is away, what do you think about?

Laura: I just worry. I'm scared.

Ann: Can you pinpoint exactly what you're afraid of?

Laura: Yeah, every noise. I mean, it's hard to say, but I read this article about a woman home alone at night and a burglar raped her. Since then I've been spooked by every little noise. I've tried to get Al to give up this work shift so he can be home more, but we can't afford to give up the money.

Ann: So you are afraid of being raped.

Laura: Yes. And the weird thing is that the story that started it was in a Christian women's magazine, about how the lady imagined Jesus comforting her while she was being raped by that burglar. I can't imagine doing that. I would just die.

Ann: You mean the woman imagined being helped by Jesus, and she wasn't afraid?

Laura:	Right. And I can't even think about it without getting scared to death.
Ann:	That's the second time you have mentioned death, Laura. Are you afraid that if you were raped, the man would kill you?
Laura:	No, that's just a figure of speech. I know that I probably wouldn't die. But I might be beaten.
Ann:	And that would be terrible.
Laura:	Yeah, but, well, it doesn't sound quite as terrible when I talk about it as when I think it.
Ann:	Let me summarize. You're afraid of being home alone at night because you might possibly be raped and beaten.
Laura:	Right!

Later, after exploring with Laura the meaning to both her and Al of her possibly being raped and beaten, Ann again summarized.

Ann:	So far you've told me that you often get frightened when you're home alone by imagining that you might possibly be raped and beaten. Then, once you get frightened, you become afraid that you will panic, and that idea just increases your fear. Also, you said you get a lot of adrenaline in your system, and that makes your hands and knees shake and your stomach flutter. You said you worry a lot once you begin to get scared. You think things like, "What would I do if that were a burglar?" Is that close to what you have told me so far?
Laura:	That sounds like me.
Ann:	What have you tried to do about your fear so far?
Laura:	I've talked with Al about giving up his shift.
Ann:	And that didn't work.
Laura:	Right. We need the money, so that's out.
Ann:	What else have you done?
Laura:	I've tried phoning friends when I'm alone at night.
Ann:	How effective has that been?

Laura:	It works for a while. But I just can't do that all the time. I have to hang up sometime.
Ann:	What else have you tried?
Laura:	I've tried to keep my mind off the fear by doing other things, or reading.
Ann:	How has . . . ?
Laura:	That's not worked at all. I keep worrying.
Ann:	Have you tried anything else?
Laura:	I don't believe so. Oh, yeah, I've tried just telling myself that I probably don't have anything to worry about.
Ann:	And that hasn't been effective?
Laura:	Not at all! This fear is not logical! It is too emotional.
Ann:	Can you think of anything else?
Laura:	No. (Pause)
Ann:	Let's see, how about planning activities away from home?
Laura:	Well, of course that works. I have a class on Tuesday and a Bible study on Wednesday. Usually by the time I get home, I'm so tired I don't stay awake long enough to get scared.
Ann:	But that doesn't do any good on the other nights.
Laura:	Right. And I can't do something every night. Besides, I *refuse* to let this fear dictate my life.
Ann:	So nothing you have tried has been a satisfactory long-term solution.
Laura:	Right. I just don't know what to do.
Ann:	It seems to me that if what you are imagining is making you afraid, then you could get over your fear if you could somehow stop imagining it.
Laura:	Yeah, it seems like it. But I don't know how to stop imagining those things.
Ann:	You mean imagining being raped and beaten?
Laura:	Yes.
Ann:	If you could change that image, then what would you change it to? What would be a more helpful image?

Laura: Let's see. (Pause) I'm having a problem. I know that "all things work together for good for those who love God," and I do love God. I just can't translate that knowledge into belief that I'll be safe.

Ann: Do you think that God can keep you safe?

Laura: Sure. But I'm not sure it's in his will.

Ann: You know, Laura, it might *not* be in his will to keep you safe. But let me tell you a story. Did you read Corrie ten Boom's *The Hiding Place?*

Laura: No.

Ann: Well, when Corrie was a little girl, she began to have some fears. Her father asked her to recall how the two of them periodically took a train trip together. He then asked Corrie how she should pay the conductor. She said something like, "Why, papa, when the conductor comes around, you give me the ticket when I need it, and I give it to the conductor." Corrie's father then said something like, "Well, that's what God is like. He gives us the ticket when we need it." So God may not have it in his will to keep you safe, but if he does test you, he'll give you the ticket. Until then, let's assume that he wants to keep you safe. We still have the problem of how you can control your fear. Now, suppose you could change the image that's causing all the fear: what would take its place?

Laura: Well, I believe that God can send a legion of angels to protect me.

Ann: How would they look? A legion of angels ringing the house, guarding you from one puny robber.

Laura: Pretty spectacular! I can imagine them, in their splendor, shining like golden light, standing arm to arm.

Ann: And on each face?

Laura: A firm jaw and a look that no one would dare challenge.

Ann: How about inside the house with you? Who's there?

Laura: Why, Jesus! I could just sit and talk to him all evening.
Ann: What would he look like?

Ann helped Laura fill in the details of the image. Then she turned the conversation to helpful Bible passages.

Ann: You know, the Bible often uses faith-building images when it is combatting fear. Just look at the wonderful imagery in the Twenty-third Psalm.
Laura: I never really noticed any imagery there, and I've known that by heart since grammar school.
Ann: Why don't you read it aloud? Here's my Bible.

Laura read the psalm aloud, and Ann jotted down some other key verses about fear for her to look up at home.[6] She also recommended that Laura use a concordance to study passages about trusting the Lord. They prepared for Laura's going home.

Ann: Before you leave, let's pray. Dear Lord. You deliver us from evil. Your mighty rod and staff comfort us. You keep us from fear and give us the courage to face whatever you bring into our lives. We pray now that you will provide a vision for Laura—that when she is home alone and begins to fear, you will fill her mind with a vision of you and your angels. You can calm her and take away her fear. You can protect her. We pray believing you will do that.

Helping People Overcome Fear
Ann did not follow the stages of helping exactly as I recommended. For example, she tried to motivate Laura to accept a new way of rethinking the problem (stage two) before she presented the new way of thinking about the problem. Usually motivating occurs as part of the action plan (stage three). We should all feel the freedom to follow the needs of our friends and not be tied to a rigid order of the five stages of counseling I discussed in chapter one. While these stages may represent the ideal progression for helping, we need not always follow the stages in order. The most effective helping is personalized to the situation.

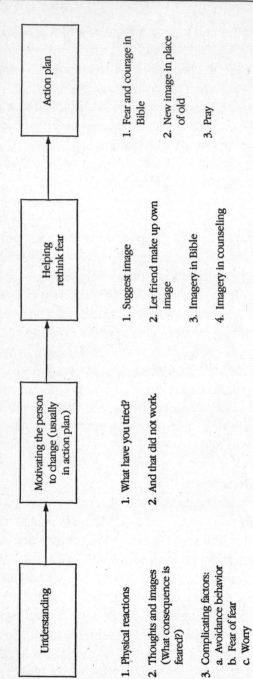

Understanding	Motivating the person to change (usually in action plan)	Helping rethink fear	Action plan
1. Physical reactions	1. What have you tried?	1. Suggest Image	1. Fear and courage in Bible
2. Thoughts and images (What consequence is feared?)	2. And that did not work.	2. Let friend make up own image	2. New image in place of old
3. Complicating factors: a. Avoidance behavior b. Fear of fear c. Worry		3. Imagery in Bible 4. Imagery in counseling	3. Pray

Figure 4.   A Plan for Helping People Overcome Fear

Figure 4 sums up how to help friends who are afraid. First, try to understand their concerns and show that you understand. Focus especially on physical reactions, thoughts and images that reveal what they fear. Discuss the meaning of the feared consequence. Next, look at complicating factors that make fear and anxiety worse.

In the second step, motivate people to be open to a new game plan by finding what actions they have already tried. Point out (gently) that none of the strategies has worked.

Now suggest a new way to think about fear. This involves replacing one image with another. Laura, for instance, created her own positive image (angels) to combat the fear-provoking image (burglar). In support of your idea, point out some well-known instances of courage imagery in the Bible. For example, we have courage when we rest in the Lord (Ps 23). Allude to how helpful imagery has been for professional counseling.

Fourth, suggest a study of Scripture that talks about fear. Suggest your friend practice the image that has been created, especially when fearful. Finally, pray that God will provide a vision that will supplant the old image, and encourage your friend to trust completely in Jesus.

What happened to Laura? God answered the prayer. He gave Laura a vision of his protection and care over her life. After several months she told Ann she had been completely healed of her fears. She gave God the glory.

8

DEPRESSION: A DOWNWARD SPIRAL

I'm depressed," said Sue, and she looked it. Her eyes were puffy from frequent crying. Her clothes were wrinkled. She wore no make-up, and her hair was not brushed. Sue seemed to be a different person from the pert thirty-year-old woman I had seen a mere two weeks ago.

"What happened?" I asked.

Her response, like most of her movements, was slow in coming. The tears came first. "George has asked me for a separation. I don't know what to do."

I was stunned. I could imagine Sue's shock. I had always considered them a happily married couple. "That's really a blow, isn't it?"

"Yeah. It just came out of nowhere. Last Tuesday we were just as happy as could be. Then Wednesday night he told me that he had met someone else. And he left that night. I've been so depressed I can't do anything. I just think about it over and over.

Now my job is falling apart. My house is a wreck. I just don't see how I can carry on."

"It sounds like you feel helpless," I said.

"Yeah," she said flatly. "That's the bad thing. I just can't do anything about it. I'm totally powerless."

How Serious Is It?

Depression is one of the most common problems in our culture. Of course, the severity of depression varies greatly, from people so depressed that they will not get out of bed, to people who show no outward signs yet say they are "a little down." One of our tasks as helpers is to estimate first how serious the depression is.

Depression is not a disease like measles that is easily diagnosed. Professionals may even disagree about whether someone is seriously depressed. But if people say they need professional help, they probably do. Even very disturbed people are usually able to determine whether they need professional help. Often the best way to judge the seriousness of depression is simply to ask.

Depressed people do not act like their normal selves. Their bodies may function differently, and they think, feel and speak differently. Of course, individuals differ, but certain signs of depression are common (see figure 5). Are many of the signs listed in figure 5 evident in your friend?

In most cases depression cures itself within two months. Staying depressed for longer than that often indicates a neurochemical imbalance. In such cases, your friend might need a physician to prescribe a drug that will restore the balance before he or she can begin to win out over depression.

Any number of common events may trigger depression. The loss of someone loved is a major cause, whether through death, divorce, separation or moving. Social rejection or unreturned love may trigger depression. What is common to every cause is this: a person's attempt to achieve goals is thwarted by what seems to be impossible obstacles. Sometimes we create those obstacles by setting up unrealistic goals: overcommitting ourselves, taking on too big a job, setting too high standards for ourselves. Other times the cause of depression may be events beyond our control—a natural disaster, a physical handicap or a bad situation we are caught in (addiction, discipline problem with children, bad marriage, unemployment and the like).

Behavioral indicators	Body symptoms	Attitude changes
Reduced motor behavior-inactivity	Disturbed bodily functions	Apathy—"don't care" attitude
Pacing	Constipation	Excessive worry
Handwringing	Dizzy spells	Inability to concentrate
Isolation	Frequent sighing	Self-condemnation
Frequent crying	Insomnia (especially awakening early and being unable to return to sleep)	Feelings of powerlessness
Reduced desire to do "fun" activities		Thoughts of being evil
	Altered eating habits	Thoughts of being worthless
	Continually sleepy or tired	Feelings of hopelessness
	Loss of interest in sex	Complaining
	Weight loss	Feelings of anger
		Reports of suffering
		Distress
		Sadness

Figure 5. Signs of Depression

Of Leaking Pipes

Unrealistic goals are the more common problem, but not too long ago I found myself on the brink of depression because of one of those uncontrollable events. It all began when I opened the water bill: There it was—$246.16! My stomach became suddenly hollow. "This is terrible," I thought. "It can't be. There's no way we can pay this much. There's no way we could have used this much water!"

A flood of relief washed over me. (You will notice how I thought in terms of water metaphors.) "Yes, that's right! We couldn't have used this much water." I felt better already. But all the same, I was probably the first customer on the phone to the

Water Department the next morning.

"Hello. I seem to have a mistake on my water bill this month," I began.

A short silence met my tentative opener. I could almost hear her thinking, "Ho-hum. It's only 8:01 a.m. Sigh." Then she said, "Just a minute. I'll get your records." She did not seem properly sympathetic.

In a minute I heard her laughing as she picked up the phone. "I can't understand why you think there is something wrong with that bill." Still laughing, she went on, "Seriously, I'm sure there's some mistake. I'll have your meter reread. Call back in one week."

I was relieved. But, . . . a week? What if we do have a leak? No. We couldn't have a leak that big. But I did call back one week later. "Oh, did you find the mistake?" I asked confidently.

"Sir (the tone was ominous), you have a big problem." At that point I knew I was in trouble. "We reread your meter. You owe $246.16. You have a major leak."

"Oh." I was stunned.

"Either the leak is in the house, which is unlikely if you haven't noticed it, or in the pipes in the yard. If the leak is in the pipes, it may be on the city's side of the meter or on your side. Judging by the lengths of pipes involved, the chances are overwhelming that the leak belongs to you."

My mind froze. All I could think of was that the past week had cost my wife and me a mere $61.54. But we had not been idle during that week. We had called a plumber and discovered that if the leak were in our yard, he would gladly bring in a backhoe and dig up the front yard. Have you ever seen a backhoe? They look like something out of H. G. Wells's *War of the Worlds.* They devour lawns. Now ordinarily I am not *that* attached to my lawn. As it happened, though, I had just that week put my house on the market because our family was soon to move. The prospect of seeing the backhoe-monster crassly belching smoke and gnawing away at our lawn made shivers run down my spine.

I felt caught between the devil and the deep blue sea (another water metaphor). I did not even know how to pray. I somehow could not see myself pleading with God, "Please, God, make the leak be on the city's side." What to do? Frankly, I didn't know. I was up the creek without a paddle, adrift in a sea of hopelessness—helpless, powerless. This event, beyond my control, was ruining my life.

Finally, we simply asked God to somehow "heal" that leak. Shortly after praying we called a plumber to see if he could locate the leak. He discovered instead that the water meter was malfunctioning. God had healed that leak his own way. Needless to say, that cured my depression. Would that all cases "cured" so easily.

Impossible Goals

Although uncontrollable events do precipitate depression, depression more often comes from our inability to reach the goals we impose on ourselves—goals that are impossible to achieve. Has your depressed friend perhaps bought into one of these unrealistic goals? (1) Everyone should like me. (2) I should never get angry, and even when (if) I do, I should be able to control my anger. (3) I should be able to control all negative feelings. (4) I should be a perfect mother, loving wife, saint and everything else. (After all, that's what it says in Proverbs 31, right?) (5) I should be able to make him (or her) love me. (6) I should be able to control the fifteen major projects I am currently involved with. (After all, I've said no to the last three people who have asked me to do something.)

There are three points to notice about these unrealistic goals. First, they *are* unrealistic. Yet we demand them of ourselves. Second, they each involve the word *should* (or *must*, or *have to* or *need to*). Third, we expect terrible consequences if we fail to reach the goals. These unrealistic "shoulds," with catastrophic consequences when we fail, make us feel under extreme pressure.

How do people respond when they meet an obstacle to their

goal? They try harder. They think, "Try a little harder. You can do it. Just a little more effort." Their bodies produce adrenaline, keying them up for greater efforts. Sometimes they become angry at the obstacle. Anger helps us get our way when we are frustrated (1 Kings 21). Often, goals are attained with this terrific onslaught of activity. The frenzy, the panic, the energy, gets results. Having been rewarded for our efforts, we will do it again and again.

But sometimes obstacles remain unmovable. Depending on their past experience, people may push even harder. But sometimes even the greatest effort will not move that mountain. Then people become angry with themselves, hoping to motivate themselves to work harder. Finally, deciding that the obstacle is indeed unmovable, they become depressed. Their behavior changes, often dramatically. They quit trying to reach their goal or (sometimes) *any* goal. Some people despair of life. Depressed people often quit doing routine jobs. They do not feel that they deserve to have any fun. They also begin to think differently: "It's hopeless. I'll never reach that goal. What's the use of trying? I'm powerless." They feel sad, ashamed, guilty. They talk about their feelings, and tears are never far from the surface.

An interesting parallel to depression as I have described it occurs in some famous experiments. Martin Seligman placed dogs in a box with a barrier down its center.[1] The barrier prevented the dogs from easily moving from one side to the other, but with some effort the dogs could leap over the barrier. Seligman turned on a signal, and then shocked the dogs' feet. It did not take the dogs long to learn that if they jumped the barrier at the signal, they were no longer shocked.

Other dogs faced a similar task except that the barrier was built so high that the dogs could not escape the shock. After a while those dogs did not even try to escape. As soon as the signal preceding the shock came on, the dogs laid down on the floor, whining and crying until the shock was turned off. The dogs acted the way depressed people act. It is a "learned helplessness." Since Seligman's experiments, learned helplessness has been discovered in rats, sheep, pigeons, and monkeys as well as humans. In fact, one of psychology's most prestigious journals recently devoted a whole issue to the idea that human depression is due to learned helplessness.[2] Substantial evidence supports the argument, but it is not conclusive.[3]

Seligman says that learned helplessness occurs when we determine that what we do has no effect on what happens. This is true both when uncontrolled events assail us and when we set unreasonable goals for ourselves. Once we decide that a situation is hopeless, we become sad and stop trying to reach our goal. Enter complications. As we less frequently try to reach our goals, we fall behind on ordinary tasks. This adds more pressure to seemingly hopeless situations. A vicious circle results: The more depressed we feel, the more behind we get, which leads to more depression.

Other complications arise because our thoughts change.[4] Things that go wrong attract attention. Thus, when we are depressed we think about our problems: "I'm helpless. I'm never going to catch up. I feel so bad. Why do I feel so blue? I should be able to snap out of this. I must be a terrible person for not being able to control this depression. This is terrible. Woe is me." Such thoughts keep us depressed, and if by some chance we begin to conquer our depression, the negative thoughts may plunge us back into "the pits."

Depression is a downward spiral, begun by loss of control and made worse by lack of energy and negative thinking. It is a maelstrom that sucks us ever downward.

Projects Due . . . and Other Failures

Roberta and Ed were students. Near the end of a pressure-filled semester, while on a mid-afternoon break at a local eatery, they discussed school. Roberta confided to Ed that she felt depressed. She was twenty-two years old and, after working three years, had returned to school to complete her degree in journalism, a highly competitive field. Ed, twenty-six years old, was a graduate student in physics. He attended a local church and volunteered some time each week at a church-based counseling service provided by lay counselors and supervised by a pastor.

They discussed two major topics: what Roberta's depression felt like and what caused it. This conversation is characteristic of stages one (understanding) and two (helping rethink the problem). Notice how the stages are intimately linked together as Ed helps Roberta identify her thoughts and feelings of loss of control.

Ed: Now, Roberta, you say you are depressed and anxious. What is it like when you are depressed? I know that it's not always the same, so tell me about the last time you felt depressed. When was that?

Roberta: Well, you mean . . . when I felt really bad? (Ed nods.) Okay, I guess it was last night.

Ed: Uh-huh. And what happened last night? Try to imagine yourself back in that situation. What time is it?

Roberta: About midnight.

Ed: Now, what was happening? Tell me as if you were seeing a movie run through your mind. You can just narrate the movie to me. What happened last night?

Roberta: Well, . . . I had been thinking about this big project we have due next Wednesday. I mean . . . I'd been thinking most of the day that I wasn't going to be able to get it done. I mean, I'd get something in, but it wouldn't be any good because I'd been so depressed that I hadn't been able to work on it. I tried, but every time I tried, my hands started shaking like this (holds up a hand that is visibly shaking). I mean, how can I type like this? And besides . . .

Ed: So you didn't think you could get your hands to stop shaking enough to type. (She nods.) That sounds like you didn't believe you could really control your emotions.

Roberta: I can't! And, like I was going to say, when I start to type

I just start thinking how the project isn't going to be any good and how I'll just start crying anyway and before too long I *will* just start crying.

Ed: You really are having a tough time controlling your emotions.

Roberta: I sure am. (Eyes fill with tears)

Ed: So you think a couple of things and you become upset. You think that you won't be able to control your hands, and you think you won't be able to stop yourself from getting depressed and crying. Oh, and you think that you want the project to be good, but your depression is stopping you from doing as well as you'd like.

Roberta: Exactly. (Sighs) I get mad at myself for not being able to get a hold of myself. I've always been able to kind of bounce back before, but this time I . . . Well, I just can't. And I ought to be able to.

Ed: You also disappoint yourself because it seems that you're helpless to control this thing.

Roberta: Right. I can't control it. And I get angry and that just makes it worse because I can't do it.

Ed: Do what?

Roberta: You know. Can't control my emotions.

Ed: Sounds like you think it's hopeless.

Roberta: Yeah, pretty much.

Ed's strategy has been to show Roberta that he understands what she is thinking, feeling and doing. In particular, he has drawn her attention to her helpless, hopeless and powerless thoughts. Their talk continued much the same for twenty-five more minutes. During that time Roberta mentioned several concerns, including a terminally ill family member, an unquenchable ambition, a fear of physical illness and a male-female relationship that was not proceeding as she would like.

In each case, Ed drew her attention to the hopelessness of the situation. Then he asked Roberta if he could tell her about a psychology experiment that he had read about. She agreed, and

Ed told her about Seligman's experiments.

Ed: Can you identify in any way with these dogs?

Roberta: I sure can. I feel like I'm having the same thing happen to me.

Ed: How do you mean?

Roberta: Well, I mean, they couldn't really stop bad things from happening, and I can't either.

Ed: It sounds the same way to me, and that's why I shared the experiment with you. Your physical problem, your relative's illness, your disappointment with Frank's decision to date others, your inability to control your nervousness or sadness—all of these things seem to suggest that you are feeling out of control in some parts of your life.

Roberta: Yeah, I don't have much control over my life. How can I get control?

Roberta felt out of control. Despite having a lot going for her, she believed herself to be totally helpless. Having worked as a paraprofessional counselor, Ed encouraged Roberta to seek help at the counseling service at which he volunteered. Then, under the supervision of a pastor with years of counseling experience, Roberta's counselor helped her fight her way out of the pit while Ed provided the support of a friend.

9

HELPING THE DEPRESSED

What can be done about depression? How can this whirlpool be reversed to push depressed people upward and out of the pit? If people become depressed because they feel they have lost control, then depression can be reversed if they regain their feelings of control. At first, progress is slow, painfully slow. But then, bit by bit, people are pulled out of depression; and the farther up they go, the more their momentum pulls them up. They can prevent future depressions by maintaining a sense of control. So far so good.

What is not obvious is *how* to restore feelings of control.

Seligman had trouble with his "depressed" dogs. First, he removed the barrier that kept them from the safe (unshocking) side. All the dogs had to do was walk, run or crawl across the box and they would receive no additional shocks. Of course, the dogs did not know that. Thus, when the dogs were signaled that shock was about to occur, they cowered on the floor and began to cry and whine and, in general, act helpless. Imagine how that behavior would look to someone unfamiliar with the dogs' history. It would look strange, to say the least. As we attempt to help people who are depressed, we need to remind ourselves that what looks to us like irrational behavior probably makes sense to the person who is depressed.

Seligman tried to persuade his dogs to move across the cage. If he could get the dogs to move to an area of no shock, then they could learn to escape or avoid the pain. Seligman used social encouragement to try to get the dogs to move: he called; he whistled; he pleaded; he commanded. The dogs did not budge. It was as if the dogs were thinking, "It's not time to move. Don't you see that we're suffering?"

Humans try this strategy. Wanda let it be known at church that she was feeling depressed. That week, she received two invitations to go bowling, one to help her with housework and one to go shopping. She turned all of them down. Later two friends came by individually to encourage her. Although that helped a little, the effect did not last.

When encouragement did not work, Seligman tried a more basic motivation—food. He did not feed the dogs for twenty-four hours. Then, when the dogs were acting "depressed," he placed their favorite food on the safe side of the cage. No response. In fact, to get the dogs to move, Seligman had to *drag* them across the cage. Finally, after being dragged across the cage many times, some dogs did eventually learn to avoid pain.

Now I am not recommending this sort of "drug therapy" for depressed humans. But the experiment illustrates how tenacious depression can be. It is not easy to help someone conquer depression. What helps one person will not necessarily help another; no one psychological treatment will or can work with all people. Even prayer will be ineffective for some people, for any of several reasons: the unbelief of the person prayed for (Mk 6:5-6), the insufficient faith of the one who prays (Mt 17:19-20), conflict with the will of God (1 Jn 5:14), or even being in a wrong relationship with another person (1 Pet 3:7). Effective helping means being open to trying several routes.

Earlier I asked, How can people regain a feeling of control? It begins when they *systematically attack the behaviors and thoughts that keep depression going.* Our job as helping friends is to help in that attack.

Get Busy!

People in the grip of depression need to pursue some goal whether they feel like it or not. First, help them meet the routine demands of their lives. Instead of their saying, "I'll let this housework go," or "I won't mow the lawn this weekend," or "I'll answer these letters next week," they need to accomplish *something* immediately. Help them choose one small task. Only after success should they attempt a second. By doing some small, manageable task, depressed people help themselves in several ways. They slow down build-up of pressures. They demonstrate that they are in control of at least one area of life. (Depressed people tend to focus on the one area where they are least effective while ignoring all the areas in which they are doing fine.) In *doing* a task they also are forced to think about something besides their troubles.

In my church several women happened to become depressed at about the same time. Other women in the church banned together to help these depressed women with routine housework. In each case the depressed women pitched in as well, forced out of their lethargy. This was a very real help. It wasn't as glamorous as counseling, but in several cases it was just as effective.

Second, help them have fun. When people become depressed, they often feel that it is wrong to have fun. Maybe they don't believe they could enjoy themselves. Maybe they "can't afford the time" to have fun. Maybe they feel too sinful or guilty to deserve any fun—a kind of self-punishment or self-condemnation. But when they took fun out of life, their entire world became problem oriented. To kick depression they must open their world again to laughter and enjoyment.

One depressed friend found that by going sailing on Saturday afternoons he could shed the cares of his week. His wife escaped by attending garage sales on Saturdays. She got her children Christmas presents in July, and she was happier for it.

Think Right

D. Martyn Lloyd-Jones once wrote of depression that our problem is we *listen* to ourselves rather than *talk* to ourselves.[1] When we are depressed, we think thoughts that keep us that way. To break out of depression, we must consciously and systematically talk to ourselves in a different way.

Our thoughts and our emotions are intimately linked. For example, imagine yourself walking down the street. A man approaches, stumbling and weaving drunkenly. You swerve right to allow him to pass, but as you swerve, so does he. As he reaches out and grasps your arm, he looks into your face and in a labored way says, "Help me. I'm a diabetic. Get me to a doctor."

If you really walked into this fantasy, I suspect that your emotional reaction to the man changed sharply when you found out he was a diabetic rather than a drunk. In other words, your thoughts about a drunk person produced one emotional reaction, and your new thoughts about a diabetic produced another. Thoughts affect emotions.

Depressed people need to "talk" to themselves so that they can change their thinking and thus change their depression. We bring about many changes in our lives by changing our thoughts. For example, when I was learning to drive, my father took me to a cemetery with winding roads. (I don't even want to think about why he chose a cemetery.) He sat me in front of the steering wheel and gave me basic instructions about driving with a manual transmission. Then he settled back to serious prayer while I tried to coax that big 1959 Ford into motion.

One of the hardest parts was turning the motor on. For some

strange reason, every time I turned the ignition the car leaped forward. I would wail and gnash my teeth while Dad prayed fervently. Before long I began to think, "Why are you jumping around, car? Oh yes, I must remember to push in the clutch *before* I turn the key. See! It worked! That was easy. Now what do I have to do? Put the gear into first. Now let the clutch out. Oops! It died. I didn't give it enough gas. Here we go again. Now, this time I'll give it plenty of gas. What's wrong with this clutch? I think the motor is going to blow up if the clutch doesn't engage soon. Whoa!! I'm moving. Dad, pray softer please . . ."

Learning a new skill forced me to *instruct* myself very consciously about my new behaviors. Before long, however, those thoughts became so automatic that I hardly ever notice them now. My father has almost given up praying aloud when he rides with me.

But look what happens if we try to change well-established behavior, such as driving. Suppose I went to England and began to drive on the left-hand side of the street instead of the right. Immediately I would start talking to myself again. "Okay, remember to keep left. I know I'm likely to get confused when I turn a corner. Here comes a corner now. Keep left. Good! I did a good job on that one."

This same principle operates whenever we change any well-established behavior, whether that behavior is our tennis backhand, the frequency of our Bible reading, or the thoughts and behaviors we have when we are depressed. To change our experience, we must change our thinking.

We must work continually to replace old thoughts with new thoughts. Just because I observe Jimmy Connors hit backhands on television and then tell myself that I am now going to hit a backhand like his does not mean that I will instantly hit better backhands. I need to tell myself how to improve my stroke if it is to make much difference in my game. I also need to practice hitting backhands. The same principle applies to helping people change their self-defeating thinking that is depressive. Just because people read a book or hear a tape about depression does not mean they will instantly have no more depression. Rather, they must practice continually changing their thinking to combat their depression. We help them if we can encourage them in new self-talk.

Most people have tried to think their way out of depression—and failed. Why? One reason is that they try once or twice, then throw up their hands and quit.

But this is not the only reason people fail to control their thoughts and depression. People sometimes change their thoughts to other unhelpful thinking, like, "Don't be depressed. I've just got to kick this depression. I must get out of this terrible slump. Now there I go again getting depressed."

Why does this kind of thinking not relieve depression? To a depressed friend, I might say, "Okay, Al, do what I say. Now *don't* think about oranges. *Don't* think about how they feel in your hand. *Don't* think about how orange they are, or about how they squirt juice when you peel them. And above all, *don't* think about how oranges taste." Of course, when I have done this, people usually visualize oranges and begin to salivate.

Yet when they tell themselves, "Don't be depressed," they wonder why they get depressed. In reality, commanding oneself not to be depressed (afraid, angry or whatever) is like ordering oneself to be depressed (afraid, angry or whatever). The person is entirely focused on the problem. To stop depression, the person must get his or her mind off the problem.

Another reason people may fail to think their way out of depression is that they rely on repetition: "I'm going to be happy. I'm going to be happy. I'm going to be happy . . ." Such repetition does not usually help, no matter how good the intention. After a couple of repetitions, the commands lose their force.

So how should they think if new thinking is to work? First, realize that depression is a process rather than an event. We do not become depressed in the same way that we have an accident, that is, all at once. There are definite stages to depression. First

Bible Passage

2 Corinthians 10:3-5 For though we live in the world we are not carrying on a worldly war, for the weapons of our warfare are not worldly but have divine power to destroy strongholds. We destroy arguments and every proud obstacle to the knowledge of God, and take every thought captive to obey Christ.

Principle

We can use an image of storming a stronghold to capture our thoughts and focus them on God. We apparently overthrow literal strongholds in the unseen world when we fix our minds on obedience to Christ.

Isaiah 26:3 Thou dost keep him in perfect peace, whose mind is stayed on thee, because he trusts in thee.

Trusting in God should be the focus of our attention. God honors this by granting us perfect peace.

Romans 7:24-25 Wretched man that I am! Who will deliver me from this body of death? Thanks be to God through Jesus our Lord! So then, I of myself serve the law of God with my mind, but with my flesh I serve the law of sin.

Concentrate on the deliverer, Jesus himself. Picture him. Picture yourself shielded by his might.

1 Thessalonians 5:16-18 Rejoice always, pray constantly, give thanks in all circumstances; for this is the will of God in Christ Jesus for you.

Even though we get depressed we can be glad that God works in all things for good for those who love him, who are called for his purpose (Rom 8:28 paraphrased).

Philippians 4:8-9 Finally, brethren, whatever is true, whatever is honorable, whatever is just, whatever is pure, whatever is lovely, whatever is gracious, if there is any excellence, if there is anything worthy of praise, think about these things. What you have learned and received and heard and seen in me, do; and the God of peace will be with you.

Focus on God's character. Think about good things and do something good.

Figure 6. Thoughts That Can Beat Depression

hints of depression come when people anticipate events that might make them feel helpless. At the second stage signs of depression begin to be noticed. The third stage is full-blown depression. At each stage people *can think* things that will help them avoid the whirlpool of depression.

In figure 6 are five biblical passages that suggest thoughts that help people avoid or defeat depression. For example, people may imagine themselves successfully managing their depression. They may imagine God in all of his glory and all the quality of his character. They may trust in God as the giver of peace and in Jesus as the deliverer from depression. Our best help is to get depressed people focusing their attention on the Source of solution rather than on the problem.

Psalm 42 tells of a man dealing with depression. It is almost as if the depressed part of the man is arguing with the healthy part as he resists depression.

[1]As a hart longs for flowing streams,
   so longs my soul for thee, O God.
[2]My soul thirsts for God,
   for the living God.
When shall I come and behold
   the face of God?
[3]My tears have been my food day and night,
   while men say to me continually,
"Where is your God?"
[4]These things I remember,
   as I pour out my soul:
how I went with the throng,
   and led them in procession to the house of God,
with glad shouts and songs of thanksgiving,
   a multitude keeping festival.
[5]Why are you cast down, O my soul,
   and why are you disquieted within me?
Hope in God; for I shall again praise him,
   my help [6]and my God.

My soul is cast down within me,
   therefore I remember thee
from the land of Jordan and of Hermon,
   from Mount Mizar.
7Deep calls to deep at the thunder of thy cataracts;
   all thy waves and thy billows have gone over me.
8By day the LORD commands his steadfast love;
   and at night his song is with me,
   a prayer to the God of my life.
9I say to God, my rock:
   "Why hast thou forgotten me?
Why go I mourning
   because of the oppression of the
   enemy?"
10As with a deadly wound in my body,
   my adversaries taunt me,
while they say to me continually,
   "Where is your God?"
11Why are you cast down, O my soul,
   and why are you disquieted within me?
Hope in God; for I shall again praise him,
   my help and my God.

In the first three verses, the psalmist expresses the depth of his depression. He is so depressed that he longs for death and cries "night and day." But in verse 4 he begins to cope with his depression. He reminds himself of what God has done in his life. In verses 5 and 6, he actively questions his depression. In addition, he reminds himself to hope in God, to praise God and to remember that God is his help. In verse 7, he remembers the power of God, and in verse 8 he prays. Verses 9 and 10 remind us that merely doing these things one time does not eliminate depression; his doubts return. But in verse 11, the psalmist again questions whether his suffering is really worth comparing with his life in God. He again looks to the omnipotent God of heaven for help.

Read the psalm with your depressed friend, pausing occasionally to personalize the thought: How has God helped you in the
past (v. 4)? Why are *you* depressed (v. 5)? Can you hope God will
help you this time (v. 5)? And so on. Your probing encouragement will direct him or her to the true Help.

The psalmist has enlisted the perfect cure for depression. He
invokes the power of the all-powerful God. Even though people
may feel (and may actually be) powerless in a situation, God is
not powerless. Furthermore, he wants us to ask him for help.

I marvel at God's wisdom. He did not need to institute prayers.
He could have read our minds and acted on that knowledge. In
fact, God knows what we need before we even ask (Mt 6:8). Yet
in his wisdom God lets us pray for our needs. In so doing, he
demonstrates his care, allows us to reaffirm our reliance on him,
and builds our faith by answering our prayers. We have a wise
and a wonderful God.

An Overall Plan

Helping the depressed is not easy. Seligman's dogs seemed almost to prefer their pain. Our efforts may also be met with resistance or even anger or claims that our ideas are futile and cannot
work.

Yet we want to help if we can. Loving makes us want to try.
In figure 7 we can see graphically some of the steps to take.

First we must spend time, lots of it, trying to understand what
depressed people believe to be the cause of the depression.
Notice the instances when they felt a loss of control, and repeat
or paraphrase those instances. As they realize that they feel out
of control, ask them how they think they might re-establish control. Spend time discussing how they intend to change their
thoughts and behaviors. Encourage them to put the plans into
effect and to discuss with you later how they worked.

Often I ask depressed people if we can pray together, and tell
them that, although they feel out of control, I know that God is
not out of control. When I am with people who are not Christian,

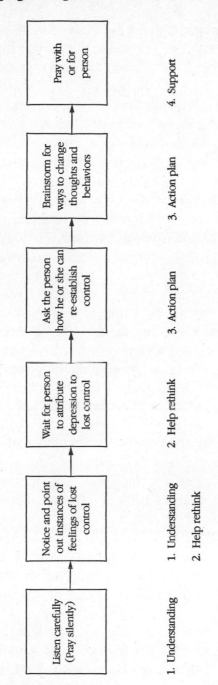

Figure 7. Helping a Depressed Person

I may or may not offer to pray *with* them, but I always try to pray *for* them. I will say something like, "I don't know what you think about the power of prayer, but I really think God answers prayer. So I would like to pray for you. I know that God can take your depression away. I hope you don't mind my praying for you." No one has yet said they minded, though some people have merely interpreted that as my way of expressing support. But telling them makes it easier to give the glory to God when the prayer is answered.[2]

Help them gain control over habits. One way that people who are depressed keep themselves depressed is by deciding that their problems are caused by their personality traits. They think of themselves as worthless, perfectionistic, unlovable and even as having a chronically depressed personality. When people reason like that it is impossible for them to try to change. How can anyone change his or her personality? How can they make fundamental alterations in traits when they hardly have the energy to survive? Somehow we must dislodge people from this way of thinking so that they can do something to ease the pressure that has accumulated.

Bill, a friend of mine, was once depressed. He habitually described himself as perfectionistic, which made his depression worse. Every time he fell short of a goal, it strengthened his perception that he was doomed to perpetual depression.

I set as my goal to help him see one thing differently: that what he called perfectionism was merely a habit of thinking. Although this seems such a fine distinction that it is almost not worth making, it is actually a crucial distinction. He couldn't see how he could change the way he was (perfectionistic). But he had changed a number of troublesome habits. He had given up smoking about five years earlier, and he had reduced his swearing when he took his present job in management.

First, I encouraged Bill to talk about all the times he acted perfectionistically. He could name a few, but not many. I didn't try to refute him, but whenever I mentioned his behavior I referred to it as behaving perfectionistically rather than as his being perfectionistic. Then I casually asked whether he had *ever* acted in a way that showed a tolerance of his own shortcomings. He could think of a few times, which I had him describe in detail. After he finished describing about three instances, I remarked that it sounded as if he had not always behaved perfectionistically, but had recently gotten in the habit of being intolerant of his failings. He agreed, and I mentioned that habits are sometimes difficult to break. I said that some people could *never* break a habit, but others could—if they put their mind to it. That got him talking about how he stopped smoking.

I saw Bill about a week later after church. He pulled me aside and said that during the past week, he had decided that he was strong enough to break this bad habit of negative thinking. Having made that decision, he had felt as if chains that had recently held him back in his business had simply fallen away. He had been a virtual dynamo at work during the last part of the week.

For Bill, his fear of failure, which he called perfectionism, was keeping him depressed and lethargic. Being freed to think about the problem differently helped him change his behavior drastically.

A second way to help people control their behavior is to help them set reasonable goals rather than impossible ones. Sandy had been depressed for weeks. She had spent much of her time in bed, listless. She had even gone to a psychologist who was seeing her twice weekly. Still she remained depressed. She had fallen behind on several major projects in school, and the semester was nearing completion. For two months she had looked forward to meeting a friend from undergraduate days in Washington, D.C.—about a two-hour drive from Richmond. Yet, as the date approached, she felt that she would have to cancel because of the pressures of school. Sandy complained to Lori, her roommate. Lori said, "What do you think will happen if you stay home all weekend to work on your project?"

With a sigh Sandy said, "Well, I'll try to get it done."

"You don't sound very confident that you'll get it done."

"I know that I ought to be able to get it done . . ."

"But?"

"But, I know realistically that it's probably hopeless," said Sandy.

"Why?" asked Lori.

"Because . . . I just seem to waste time. If I get more depressed, I just go to bed. So I'll probably spend all weekend in bed, depressed. That's the way it's been all semester."

"Look. About how much work do you have left, in terms of time, if you worked hard on the project?"

"Probably twelve to fifteen hours of solid work," Sandy sighed.

"What if you worked really hard for a fixed amount of time tonight and tomorrow morning and then you reward yourself by taking the rest of the weekend off?"

"You mean, whether or not I finish the project?"

"You said it was due Thursday, right? Will you have any time to work on it Monday, Tuesday or Wednesday? Then why don't you set a time? Work hard for that amount of time, and then reward yourself."

"That sounds like a good idea. I can work about four hours tonight and about four tomorrow—and still be off by noon!" Sandy exclaimed.

During the weekend Sandy worked on Friday night and even stayed up late. She worked again on Saturday morning and had accomplished far more than she had anticipated. At noon she left for Washington, D.C., where she had a fine weekend, free from depression and guilt.

Help them gain control over thoughts. To help people control their thoughts, we must first help them become aware of the thoughts. Ron, a manager of a restaurant, has been talking to Sidney, his assistant manager. Sidney has talked about how little control he feels. He complains that he gets particularly exasperated with his wife, Clare, who has made him so angry that at times he has even hit her. After getting Sidney to describe the most recent incident, Ron asks him whether he has lost his temper with Charles, his eight-month-old son who cries a lot.

"No! He doesn't know any better," answered Sidney.

"It sounds like you are saying that you get angry with Clare and even hit her when you think, 'She ought to know better.' But when you are angry at Charles, you think, 'He doesn't know any better,' and you control your temper."

"I never thought of it like that, but . . . yeah, when I think one thing I lose my temper, but when I think something else I keep control."

Ron asked, "Do you think the same thing might be happening with your moods?"

"It could be! Maybe I do think myself into these depressions."

"How could you find out?"

After a short pause Sidney said that he didn't know.

"Well," Ron continued, "some people keep a diary. When they notice they're getting depressed, they tune into their thoughts, something like having a third ear that can hear what they're thinking. Then they jot down a note to themselves about their thoughts."

"That sounds like a good idea," replied Sidney. "I usually carry a pad anyway. I'll just see if I can keep track of what I'm thinking."

About ten days later Sidney and Ron are again talking after work. Sidney steers the conversation to his list of thoughts. He had found four types of thought that resulted in depression. First, he felt that he was not doing as well in his career as he would like. Second, he was unable to control his temper as well as he thought he should. Third, thoughts of his failing marriage depressed him. Fourth, feelings of weakness because of his inability to control his depression made him sad.

Once Sidney had identified the thoughts making him blue, he was able to interrupt those thoughts and concentrate on other things. As a way of changing his preoccupation with his marriage and career, he resumed regular Bible study after a hiatus of over three years. In time he mastered his depression, and he and Clare entered counseling to work on their marriage problems. Ron helped them find a good counselor.

Help them set goals. Donna and Beth talked on the phone each day. Donna had slid into depression with the birth of her third child almost a year ago. She always felt behind in her housework and was exhausted. The baby seemed unhappy all the time. Her oldest girl was functioning well in the second grade, but the middle child, Meg, was overly demanding.

Beth, a mother of three somewhat older children, helped Donna realize that such stages were only temporary—even if they seemed like they were going to last forever. Beth related a similar instance of depression after the birth of her youngest child, a "surprise package from the Lord." Beth told Donna that what had helped her pull out of despair was planning some limited goals, for one week at a time. Beth told her too how she had kept track of her moods and how it had helped.

Beth: Donna, you say you want to feel better. Let's try to be as precise as we can. Suppose you think of a scale where zero equals the worst you ever felt in your life and ten equals the best you ever felt. Of course, you are going to fluctuate, sometimes feeling better and sometimes worse, but what number do you think you are near now?

Donna: I'd say zero.

Beth: So this is the worst, huh?

Donna: Yeah, of course I'm not always at zero, but . . . most of the time I am.

Beth: Well, where do you hope to be by the end of the summer? Realistically.

Donna: I guess I'd like to be at six.

Beth: That's pretty ambitious.

Donna: I guess it is but . . . well, I'm so sick of being down.

Depressed people commonly set goals either too high or too low. They reason like Donna, or they say, "It's hopeless. I'll never get better." Either way we need to help adjust their goal to reality.

With overoptimism, people set themselves up for failure. With overpessimism, they refuse to take responsibility for changing.

Beth suggested a relatively low goal for Donna in order to make it more likely that she would succeed. She also tried to use a vivid word-picture to fortify Donna as she began. During the early stages of battling depression, sometimes little progress occurs.

Beth: Donna, I suppose if I were to set a goal for you, it would be closer to two. Even that may be too optimistic. You see, depression is like an emotional roller coaster. It pulls you down, down, down. The farther down you go, the more momentum the depression seems to have. What you need to do is to step into that depression and try to stop it from going down. Try to get it to start going up. But to stop it down at the bottom, there has to be a time when you will feel like you're not making any progress. Progress seems slow at first.

Beth helped Donna choose eight small goals. The goals were specific tasks like "Sort through the baby's clothes," "Plan two special activities to do with Meg this week," and "Increase my average mood to two on a ten-point scale."

Help them control their bodies. The body is often involved in depression.[3] Our bodies affect our moods. Some depressions originate from a physical problem such as anemia, hypoglycemia, thyroid malfunction and general exhaustion. If people have difficulty conquering their depression, recommend they see a doctor for a general exam.

But sometimes the body is disturbed merely because we are depressed. The physical disturbance becomes an added stress that makes the depression seem even more uncontrollable. If people know that their particular symptoms are typical during depression, they can at least be freed from that worry.

Roberta was worried at first. "Why do I have so much trouble stopping my hands from shaking? Why am I so nervous?" she asked at one of our early counseling sessions.

"Well, when you get upset your nervous system gets turned on. It's part of your 'fight or flight' system, your sympathetic nervous system. When you get excited, like at some athletic competition, usually your face gets hot and your breath comes short, and your fingers shake and your stomach gets butterflies. Most of the time when we get excited like this we stay 'high' for a while. It's just our body getting 'psyched up' so that we can do a good job. After the excitement is over, we have an adrenaline low, when we are listless and tired. That's the way God made us, so we can do our best and then recover from our exertion. But sometimes it works against us. When we get depressed, our nervous system also gets turned on. Our breath gets short, our fingers tremble and our stomachs ache. But when we are depressed, we label these things differently. Instead of saying that we are psyched up, we say we are anxious. Then, when our body has its natural adrenaline low and we are tired and listless, we say that we are dejected, depressed and too tired to work. That just makes us more depressed. This is part of the downward spiral of depression."

"You mean that my nervousness is natural and not anything to worry about?" she asked.

"As we saw from those thoughts that you wrote down this past weekend, worry seems to keep you depressed. But at least this shows that your body is reacting normally. It is acting like most people's bodies when they are anxious and depressed. If that's true, then some of the things that have worked for others will probably also work for you. On Friday we will plan some ways to get yourself spiraling upward out of this depression."

Not only did Roberta's question allow me to assure her that her body was okay, but it also built her confidence that some of the things that worked for other people might work for her.

It takes time, but we will know there is progress if we see depressed friends begin to control their behaviors and thoughts, to set goals for themselves and to sense some control over their bodies.

10

THE PAIN
OF LONELINESS

A FABLE

Long ago, in the land of chivalry, a maiden who had many friends
and close family lived happily. Acquainted with God, she blessed
him daily for her good fortune. At times she trusted in him, but
at times she relied on herself. To increase her trust, God allowed
a dragon to come unexpectedly to the village and carry the young
maiden into the hills. Not having God's perspective (as you and
I have as we hear this story), the maiden despaired at her impri-
sonment in the dragon's keep.

Knights attempted her rescue but were slain. The maiden
chided their incompetence. Becoming impatient at her unwill-
ingness to learn total trust, God allowed her to escape back to
her own land.

Determined to avoid another such terrible capture, she built
around her the walls of a mighty fortress, made of slippery
stones. Her friends welcomed her back, but she complained
about her odious experience until they visited less often. When

they did visit, she was always busy. She became increasingly resentful because her friends had not rescued her from the dragon. In fact, she thought, even now they showed themselves to be uncaring and selfish. Besides, she expected rejection, and she did not think she could bear again the pain of lost friendship. So she built her fortress walls even higher, not thinking about her own way out. When she realized that she had walled herself in without a door, she cried aloud for help night and day. But when someone tried to help, she cast her burdensome baggage over the wall, crushing her friends and driving them away.

The maiden railed at God and man for abandoning her. Angry at God, she did not believe he could or would help, because he had not answered her every demand. Angry at her friends for not caring, she built the walls still higher each day.

Her friends knit a safety net and congregated around the fortress, which by now stretched into the heavens. They called for her to trust them and fall to safety. But fear made her hesitate. Gradually, they came less often until at last only God's Son remained. He continually pleaded for trust.

"I've never dropped anyone yet," he assured her.

"You've probably never caught anyone in as much danger as I," she countered.

Day after day she declared the risk too great.

When she died, they say, bitter herbs grew up within the fortress, and the angels wept sait rain upon the land for the lonely maiden.

Alone or Lonely?

Images of loneliness. Alienated from God. Cut off from people. Walled up inside a self-built fortress.

This much is clear: Loneliness is not the same as aloneness. Many times we are alone, but only we can make ourselves lonely.

Aloneness can occur for many reasons. People find themselves alone through no fault of their own. Jobs and job changes can create aloneness. Career demands can devour the time of a worker. People are laid off or fired. Others retire. Some change jobs, and social ties break. People become physically isolated and alone when they move to a new city or even a new section of town. Students become separated from friends through graduation, changing grade levels or simply changing class schedules. Accidents and illness claim family members and friends.

New circumstances force a rearrangement of our time and a reshuffling of friendships. Sometimes after a major life change, new friends do not develop immediately, and periods of aloneness can stretch for weeks, months, years. Failed marriages and single-parent families create aloneness too. Whereas most divorcing parents choose aloneness, children usually have it thrust on them as homes are ripped apart. Relationships seem almost as disposable for some people as toys—mere amusements until they break, when they are to be discarded.

Aloneness also happens because women usually outlive their husbands by an average of ten or more years. Widows are forced to fend for themselves at the time of life when they are least able to do it.

Sometimes people impose isolation on themselves, unwittingly. They may provoke others to reject them through obnoxious, rude, self-centered, demanding, haughty or manipulative behavior. Others isolate themselves through complaining, carping, sadness and self-pity. Their friendships are negatively charged and unpleasant. They may solicit help and then sabotage it. Their conversation is laced with "yes, but . . . ," which prevents change and frustrates even the most faithful friend. People can also physically isolate themselves, seldom venturing away from their familiar and safe, yet miserable, surroundings. They avoid dates, new activities, changes.

Yet all of these people might be happy with few if any twinges of loneliness. To be lonely, people must actively make themselves that way.

Loneliness is a widespread and serious problem today.[1] Lonely people feel that they don't have the type, quality or number of social relationships they want, which makes them sad and often bitter.[2] There are two kinds of loneliness: social and emotional.[3] Social loneliness occurs when people are unhappy because they have only one or two close friends but no acquaintances. This happens often when people move to a new city where they have no social network.

Emotional loneliness is more common. The emotionally lonely might have several acquaintances, but they have no friend that is close. They long for intimacy and feel unfulfilled and unhappy. Nor is it just a perception of the person; lonely people describe their relationships with their closest friends as not being intimate, and their friends agree.[4] The most distressed people are lonely both socially and emotionally.[5] Thus, loneliness can occur even when people are not alone, and aloneness does not mean people will be unhappy and lonely.

Lonely people often (1) are self-preoccupied,[6] (2) fail to act in new, risky ways, (3) cut others off,[7] and (4) act in ways that keep them lonely.[8] With walls like these protecting and isolating them, it is hard for others to construct bridges. We'll look at each building block in turn.

Self-Preoccupation

A self-preoccupied person will often be emotionally self-indulgent. I lived in the same house for my first twenty-two years. When I graduated from college, I left Knoxville, Tennessee, to attend graduate school in Boston. Knowing no one in Boston, I was alone.

I chose to make myself lonely. I played music with a melancholy air and listened to countless ballads about lost love, which reminded me of a girl in Knoxville. While the weather permitted, I went daily to Storrow Park, where young couples congregated. There I sat along the shore watching others have fun, thinking about the folks back home and sometimes reading love poetry—all of which made my loneliness acute. I developed an image of myself as a noble outcast and began to delve into the existentialism of Camus and Sartre and the existential psychology of Clark Moustakas and Rollo May. (Existentialism glorifies the aloneness of humans.) Soaked in self-pity and silent complaining, I spent long hours each day thinking of the injustice of my situation and of the nobleness of my choice to attend school far away from home.

Unwillingness to Risk

Rigidity, or refusing to take the risks necessary for breaking out of loneliness, often results from having been hurt in taking some risk. Usually people have tried to escape from loneliness, only to have their efforts flop. Most tries are half-hearted anyway because loneliness has sapped their energy and primed them to expect failure. After a few efforts—the tenacity of individuals differs—they conclude that trying to make friends is not worth the chance. Change is risky, for we never know what will happen if we change. Thus many people prefer the misery of loneliness—which is known—to the horror of uncertainty, the possibility of rejection. They believe failure is inevitable and disastrous. Rather than Tennyson's "It's better to have loved and lost than never to have loved at all," they believe, "It's better to have never tried than to have tried and proved oneself a failure."

This rigidity is cemented by two mental habits: living in the past and fearing. They can live in the past by dwelling on past triumphs and wishing them into the present, or by lamenting past defeats and rejections. The habit of fear can so dominate people as to paralyze them—fear of failure, fear of change, even fear of being unable to change. The last is often associated with the belief that "that's the way I am; I can't be any different."

Isolation

When people cut themselves off from others, they virtually guarantee loneliness. They deaden their emotions as they consciously or unconsciously harden their feelings about others. Some people become emotionally hard by denying all feelings, imprisoning themselves within stone-cold walls. Others make themselves emotionally hard by letting some feelings be especially prominent while denying others. This often happens in marriages that have gone sour. A disgruntled husband may only allow himself to feel hate, anger, resentment and disappointment toward his spouse. If warm feelings arise, he quickly shifts his attention until he can find something that will again justify negative feelings. In the end the emotions that are not exercised atrophy, like unused muscles.

People cut others off through judging and blaming. They rush to blame God for their problems. Whenever possible they blame others. At the root of their blaming lie two attitudes which are almost always present in relationship difficulties—bitterness and unforgiveness. People become bitter when they find (or think they find) others unwilling or unable to meet their needs.

The lonely person wails, "I always went out of my way to help her, yet when I got into trouble, she didn't lift her finger to help me. In fact, not a single person in the church offered to help me when I really needed it." Thinking this, our friend feels self-righteously martyred. A variation says, "I've been a faithful Christian for twenty-seven years. I can't see why God has brought this misfortune on me." The lonely person may also feel guilty: "Nobody will help me. Since my husband died, I'm not good for anything." A variation of this reasoning goes, "God must be trying to correct my sinful life by bringing all this grief to me. I'm not really good for anything." Whether people see themselves as martyrs or as guilty, as the wronged or the wronging, they cut themselves off from others. They withdraw.

Another way people isolate themselves is through pre-emptory rejection. Like a nation armed with nuclear weapons, people can launch a pre-emptory strike if they think they are in danger of being rejected. By rejecting first, they are assured that "the enemy" is hurt, even though in the end they cause their own rejection too. The friendship is terminated, and both parties are "nuked," rejected. The lonely maiden of the fable criticized her friends until they no longer returned to help.

People also isolate themselves by visualizing themselves as different from others. The differentness can take any form: more sensitive, not as smart, more shy; or, conversely, less sensitive, smarter, too outgoing. If people see themselves as in essence different, they have precluded any cure. It is hard to change who one is. The differentness provides a ready explanation for anything that happens and a ready excuse for not trying to change.

Paul Tournier, who combines existential philosophy with Christian hope, believes that people are lonely because a spirit of competitiveness pervades our culture.[9] People demand independence, the freedom to live their own life. They seek happiness as if it were something to be owned. They demand justice, equality and rights. Yet they misunderstand their deepest needs. Instead of competitiveness, they need community; instead of independence, cooperation; instead of possessing happiness, sharing happiness; and instead of rights, love. In short, the Christian existentialists—whether Paul Tournier or Bruce Larsen and Keith Miller[10]—say that the answer to loneliness is community and love.[11] The problem is isolation and separation; the solution is relatedness.

These writers are essentially correct, for we were created for relationship with God and people and for meaningful work. But helping the lonely is not so simple as merely telling them—or even letting them discover for themselves—that they must stop being self-preoccupied, rigid and rejecting. It may help us, however, to at least pinpoint for ourselves why they are lonely.

Missing Social Skills

Lonely people find it hard to form and keep close friendships. The may talk about themselves inappropriately, act self-focused or give too much unasked-for assistance.

Knowing how much we should talk about ourselves is a problem for all of us. Lonely people, though, seem to have more trouble with this than others. Early on in a relationship, when people are first meeting, they may talk about themselves too intimately. In a conversation with a stranger, they may reveal personal details of their lives. The stranger is driven away, feeling uncomfortable with such intimacy. When a relationship gets well established, however, lonely people are often reluctant to disclose personal details of their struggles and their joys. Usually men share less intimately than women, but lonely men are more closed than men who are not lonely. Women who are lonely are also reluctant to share their lives. They may perceive themselves as good listeners, but when they rarely share their own inner life, relationships begin to shrivel.

Lonely people's self-focus comes out in their conversations. They pay more attention to their feelings than to their partner's. They often talk in ways that drive people away. They ask fewer questions of their friends than nonlonely people. They are more likely than others to change topics. The lonely, more often than the nonlonely, give advice, suggestions and instructions. Perhaps they do so because they are more attuned to themselves and what *they* would do than they are sensitive to their friends' reactions. These conversational habits, coupled with feelings of shyness and mistrust, can add up to making their friends perceive them as wrapped up in themselves.

Just helping lonely people find a friend—or even becoming the friend ourself—will not always solve their problem of feeling lonely. We have to help them work on their ways of understanding the world and their relationship to God and others. We might even have to help them improve their friend-making and friend-maintaining skills.

11

DEFEATING LONELINESS

Helping defeat loneliness involves work on four fronts. All four must be understood and rethought. First, lonely people's faith needs strengthening, for they generally do not believe that God will provide all our needs. Second, their actual aloneness must be decreased so that they have a chance for social contact and intimacy. Third, their perception of their loneliness must be countered, including their morbid self-preoccupation, rigidity and rejection of others. Finally, their habits which drive people away or inhibit close relationships must be changed.

Helpers often believe that one of these areas is the *real* problem, and they set to work in that area, neglecting the others. This is a mistake. Progress comes, but so does backsliding. To really help we must concentrate on all areas *simultaneously.* We begin by laying careful groundwork through listening and assessing what can be done (stage one).

Stage One: Understanding Loneliness

Listening. The lonely often feel abandoned, isolated, alienated, rejected. They might not perceive our efforts to befriend them as helpful. They likely think that no one wants to or is able to help. So prepare to be unappreciated. If you suggest that you are helping them, they will probably be genuinely surprised.

We need patience to deal with the lonely. We must listen and respond in ways that show we understand where they're coming from. We must practice accepting them. We can't start out trying to correct their attitudes or habits. When we do, later on, speak the truth in love (Eph 4:15), we will not only speak gently but also with understanding and tolerance.

Assessing. While we are listening to the lonely, we will have to think hard. What will break the chains of their loneliness? Is the problem due more to little *social* contact or to little *intimate* contact? We have to put aside our ideas about how much contact we need: what does *this* person need? For example, one woman might be quite content with no intimate contact, having had many happy years with her husband while he lived; now she just wants a social network. By contrast, a man might have many social contacts and a large family, yet still feel isolated. Find out what *he* attributes his loneliness to: how would he describe life if he were not lonely?

Consider the possible causes. How much of the loneliness comes from being alone (social loneliness), and how much from the person's thoughts, attitudes and beliefs (emotional loneliness)? Is he or she relying on God for deliverance?

All our assessments must be tentative. We have to check out our hypotheses with the person. If we become too fond of our own ideas, it can block our helping. It doesn't work to try to "sell" our idea to the lonely. It's easy to think, "Doesn't he see what's causing the loneliness? If he doesn't see it (my way), he is never going to get over this. I know this is the answer." If I ever find myself thinking this way, I know I'm in a power struggle with the person, and I won't be able to help until I stop insisting I'm right.

Most nonprofessional (and even some professional) helpers believe that there is one best way to help the lonely person. This is a fallacy. He or she could probably be helped by about eighty percent of the professional psychologists in town, if statistics hold.[1] You can bet that few of these psychologists will use the same approach. There are many paths to helping a person with problems. Our mission is to find one way that will work, being sure that we act in ways consistent with God's truth. We may believe that God has shown us, through Scripture or through direct revelation, how we are to help a particular person. Good. The Christian life involves learning to follow the leading of God. But we must be cautious. No one infallibly hears the voice of God. No one infallibly interprets Scripture correctly. And no one always applies Scripture correctly in each circumstance. We can be easily deceived. The heart desperately wants to be right. It is easy to use Scripture or revelation to batter someone into line with our desires. We must not abuse the Word of God.

Next we must assess how willing we are to help lonely people. Are we willing to be their chief social support? An intimate listener and helper? While God calls us to lay down our lives for others, he hasn't called us to do so for everyone. Jesus walked by the pool at Bethzatha (Jn 5:2-9) where there lay "a multitude of invalids, blind, lame, paralyzed." Yet Jesus singled out only one man to help. God may not have chosen us to help the particular lonely person whom we are talking to. We must, through prayer, discern who and how God wants us to help. It will be our most important decision. If we are in God's will to be an agent of help, God will make a way. It might cost every effort, but there will be a way.

Finally, we must assess any complicating problems. Very often the lonely are also depressed and anxious. Consider the depth of the depression and your ability to help. Try some of the ideas that are suggested in chapters six through nine. Look for fear or anxiety, and deal with it as recommended in chapter seven. Usually depression, fear, anxiety and loneliness cannot be separated, so we must deal with all of them at once.

Stage Two: Rethinking Loneliness

Strengthening faith. "There's no need for a Christian ever to feel lonely," he said, "because Christians are never really alone. All we have to do to help the lonely is restore them to a right relationship with Jesus. They will never be lonely again."

This sounds wonderful—a simple solution to a difficult problem. It may come from a pastor who does little counseling or from an evangelist who visits for a series of arousing sermons and then departs. But anyone who has tried this approach and stuck around for the results knows that it helps few people. Loneliness is not generally a problem that a quick fix will solve.

Emotional appeals or sudden insights can trigger a reversal toward health, but it takes a continued ministry to solidify the gains. It's like an infantry battalion that captures an outpost. Fierce fighting was necessary for the immediate victory, but continued fighting is necessary to keep the captured ground.

Helping the lonely likewise requires much more than simply building their faith. While faith is the cornerstone, it is not the end-all of helping. Even when Adam had a close (unfallen) relationship with God, he was lonely. And God said, "It is not good for man to be alone."

Before reaching out to help another's faith, take a personal inventory. Are we allowing God to work in our own life? When we trust in God, seek his will and pray in line with it, trusting in him, he will do great things. We then can speak with authority that God is on the job. God will keep us enthusiastic about what he is doing, and what he's doing in us can encourage another to hope for help and change.

People commonly make one of two mistakes talking about their experiences with God. Some talk too little. They believe they are witnessing to Jesus' care for them by merely living the Christian life. Maybe they are. But by not labeling themselves as Christians and by not attributing to God the marvelous things he

does for them, they let people draw their own conclusions—
which might never include God. The second mistake is to witness
in a style that offends. There is, of course, a fine line here. Some
people will always be offended by the gospel, no matter how it
is presented. However, sometimes we needlessly offend by using
words we are familiar with but others are not.

After I was released from naval service, Kirby and I were traveling in Europe. We met a lawyer and his wife, fine people who
appeared not to be Christians. We spent a day together in a city.
Periodically we discussed what God was doing in our lives.
The couple seemed to become more receptive as the day wore
on. As we were walking down the street, a well-meaning person
stopped the lawyer and asked, "Are you saved?" When he did not
reply, merely walking on, the person shouted after him, "You'd
better get saved. You are going straight to hell." Angrily the lawyer
wheeled and yelled back, "How do you know what I believe? Are
you God or something?" The street evangelist had succeeded
only in angering the lawyer. The message may have been true,
but the style was destructive.

When we give spiritual counsel to someone, we must carefully
consider why we are doing it. Do we want to justify ourselves so
we can proudly know we have given "godly counsel"? If that is
our goal, we will find ourselves speaking the truth and then
shaking our head as those we "help" ignore our counsel. If we
want the person in trouble to be helped, we will give counsel in
a way suitable to that person, a way more likely to be heeded.

Restructuring schedules. Our life is governed by the way we
occupy our time. We can help people change in their lives by
helping them modify their daily schedules. Have them make a
time budget, listing how each hour of the day was spent during
the last week. Look it over together, keeping in mind how rou-
tines might be modified to (1) reduce time spent alone, (2)
increase time spent building faith, (3) decrease time spent in self-
preoccupation, (4) decrease mindless, habitual, unproductive
routine, and (5) increase tie-building to others. Little changes in

a schedule can make big changes in people's attitudes and feelings of loneliness.

Remember that lonely year I spent in Boston after college? What freed me from my self-imposed exile from life was a relatively minor change in schedule. I moved from an apartment in Boston, where I had few contacts other than my roommate, to the dormitory at M.I.T. Then I began to play tennis for about an hour each day. Because I knew so few people, I had to hit against the backboard until I saw someone of approximately equal ability and asked him to play. That's how I met Ted Steger, who was to become my best friend and my doubles partner. Knowing Ted allowed me to meet his friends and integrated me into a social network. Playing tournament tennis that summer in New England also introduced me to several local tennis players that I played with regularly. Tennis for me opened the door to an entirely new mental outlook.

Does your lonely friend have an interest in hobbies, reading or sports that could be revitalized? For almost any activity, there are others who share the interest. You may be able to help plug him or her into a new support system.

Countering ideas about loneliness. Bruce Larson has suggested that loneliness is best understood as a gift that motivates a relationship with God and with others.[2] The pain of loneliness makes the lonely aware of their need and can be a prod to growth.

Loneliness is a problem to solve, but that's not the way most lonely people see it. They see loneliness as a condition from which they need rescue. If you suggest that there is value in loneliness even though the lonely need to solve their problem, prepare for resistance. Avoid arguing about whether loneliness is "really" good for them or whether it is "really" a problem to solve, or whether they can struggle their own way out in this instance. You cannot help them by intellectual argument. You might convince them that you are right, or at least that it is pointless to argue with you, but you will not by argument motivate them to change. More likely, they will resist your help all the more.

It is more effective to just *assume* that loneliness is a problem to solve. If you mention it at all, treat it as a working assumption, a presupposition. Presuppositions are generally difficult to challenge because they are like pre-existing facts. Sometimes you can get the presupposition across by saying, "It took me quite a while to realize what a difficult problem this is to solve," or, "How have you tried to solve this problem?"

You might be challenged. "It's not a problem to solve," the person might say. "It's just that I'm doomed to be lonely. Nobody really cares."

You might be tempted to refute such statements. Don't. Accept them as assertions of discouragement and reflect, or summarize, those feelings back to the person. You might say, "You seem discouraged." This fosters understanding and sidesteps intellectual disagreements that are counterproductive.

Expect numerous self-justifications from lonely people. They usually do not want to accept responsibility for their loneliness. They will blame God and others, and will have several logical (or not-so-logical) reasons for their inability to break out of the loneliness prison. We will have to keep plugging away to help them change their perceptions until they believe that (1) time alone is not equivalent to loneliness and that (2) loneliness is a problem they can solve.

Changing social habits. We saw in chapter ten how lonely people put people off through the ways they talk. They are too self-focused, share personally too soon with acquaintances or not enough with closer friends, and offer too much advice. How can we help a lonely friend see these difficulties without driving him away? The key is in listening to them, accepting them.

Only after we have gained people's trust through listening can we gently help them examine how they might be contributing to their problem through their behavior. Help them explore whether they are provoking others to reject them. Help them see their self-preoccupation by gently noting how they seem to feel sorry for themselves or how they make themselves emotional when they think about how unfair life seems. Use their own self-pitying words to reflect back their overinvolvement with themselves. Explore with sensitivity (not as an accusation) their rigidity and failure to take risks. Ask, "What is preventing you from getting a date?" Or, "What is stopping you from going to the party at church?" Questions like these help them see the things that block them from moving forward.

Be concrete as you phrase your question. Abstract questions like, "What is stopping you from taking more risks?" diffuse the focus and don't help. Like a nozzle on a garden hose that, when tightened, sprays water over a large area, an abstract question sprays its energy over too wide a field of potential answers. Pinpoint special activities and find out what stops people from engaging in those activities. Then see if together you can think of ways to remove the roadblocks.

Help lonely people stop cutting others off. They may need to forgive those who have hurt them. This area may likely be the highest hurdle they will have to get over. Because they do not like to take responsibility for their loneliness, they only reluctantly admit that they contribute to it. Sometimes they will admit it verbally but then act as though they are mere victims.

To help them stop cutting others off, talk about specific instances. Get to the details. "Exactly what were you thinking when you felt Gennie was rejecting you? What did you two talk about right before you had this feeling? What happened that led you to believe she did not really care?" Questions like these yield results.

Often lonely people will feel that you are rejecting them. When you sense them pulling back, building an emotional wall between you, ask about it. It might be hard. Feelings of hurt and anger are usually aroused, and most people would rather have these feelings smoothed over than deal openly with them. However, when they feel that you are rejecting them, you have the most immediate example of how they experience rejection. If

you are serious about helping, talk about this. For example, Sally
wants to help Eva but notices that Eva is pulling back from her.

Sally: Something seems to be bothering you, Eva.

Eva: It's nothing. (Surly tone of voice)

Sally: I sense that something's happened. I care about you
and want to know what's wrong.

Eva: Nothing.

Sally: You don't feel like talking about it. Perhaps it's something that doesn't concern me. If it's private, I don't
want to pry. But the way you got quiet just now, my
suspicion is that it might have something to do with
you and me. Am I off base?

Eva: No. I . . . Well, I got angry when you said that you
couldn't come over tonight.

Sally: Oh. What did you think?

Eva: Well, I thought, "Just when we were getting to be
friends, now she doesn't want to spend any time with
me." You know, Sally, I don't have any friends so it's
really hard when someone that I thought was my friend
rejects me. (Begins to cry)

Sally: I'm sorry you got hurt, Eva. I didn't mean to hurt you,
and I do want to get to know you better.

Eva: It's okay.

Sally: Do you know I value you as a friend?

Eva: Uh-huh.

Sally: You know, we've been talking about rejection some,
and it just occurred to me that it might be worthwhile
looking at how this misunderstanding developed. It
might help you see how rejection sometimes develops.

Eva: What do you mean?

Sally: Well, I did something that made you think that I was
rejecting you, right?

Eva: Uh-huh. You didn't want to come over.

Sally: What did you think about when I said that I couldn't
come tonight but that maybe sometime this week or

next we could get together?

Eva: I thought, "She really doesn't want to come over. She is just making excuses."

Sally: Why did you think that? Did I give you any reason to believe I wasn't sincere?

Eva: Not really. It's just that in the past lots of people have made excuses like that and we never did get together.

Sally: Do you know positively that in all cases these people didn't want to get together?

Eva: Not in all cases. But usually I could tell.

Sally: How could you tell? You thought I was rejecting you, but I wasn't.

Eva: Well, I guess I could have been wrong.

Sally: Look what might have happened if we hadn't talked about it. You would have been angry with me for rejecting you. And I felt like something was wrong, though I couldn't really tell what it was. We might never have got together at all! Worse yet, we might have been uncomfortable with each other the next time we got together.

Eva: I guess it could have been disastrous, jumping to conclusions like that.

Suppose people hang on to an idea that traps them in a misperception. How can you shake the idea loose? One way is to propose a test that challenges the idea.

One college student that I counseled believed that he was one of the only people on campus who did not have a girlfriend. Robert felt like an outcast, an alien. And he dealt with women in a perpetual state of panic, always believing he was inadequate. I disputed his perception for an hour—to no avail. At last I said, "Okay, you're pretty sure of your idea, aren't you?"

"Absolutely," he said. "I've spent two years seeing everyone paired up, and I believe what I see."

"If you are so sure, would you be willing to put your theory to a test?" I asked. "Some day this week at lunch?"

"What did you have in mind? I have Thursday free."

"Okay, on Thursday at lunch, find a seat on the lawn of the library. Look directly across the street at the bookstore. Would you say a lot of people would pass between you and the bookstore during that hour? What percent of the people will cross in front of you walking with someone else, and what percent will pass walking alone?"

"I'd say about ninety percent would be with someone else."

"It will be interesting to put that prediction to the test. Get a paper and pencil and sit out there on Thursday. Keep track of how many go past alone and how many are with someone. Keep track long enough to satisfy yourself that you have an accurate estimate of how people walk around campus."

The next week Robert entered my office looking sheepish. "I did the experiment," he began. "I was right about the ninety percent—only it was ninety percent who were alone rather than paired." That experiment turned Robert around. Instead of seeing himself as a pariah, he saw himself as a normal college man, and he began to relax in his dealings with college women.

One Woman's Action Plan

Rena Canipe is a living testimony to the love of Jesus Christ. At sixty-seven, she has been a widow for five years. Rena has continued a ministry that she and her husband began years ago.

Local food stores often throw away damaged goods, goods past their selling date, goods that have been dirtied by one broken bottle inside a tightly packed case of bottles. Rena got permission from the stores to share this food with shut-ins. Each morning at 5:00 a.m. she takes her car behind the stores to gather usable food. (She also cleans the premises of trash and litter.) Returning home, Rena washes the bottled goods and repackages other consumables. Then she delivers the goods to shut-ins—usually not finishing till late afternoon.

I interviewed Rena to learn some of her secrets of ministry to the lonely. I began by asking who the people were that she most regularly ministered to.

Rena: Most of the people that I help I have know through church, so they have a Christian background, though many have drifted away from their Christian foundation. Most are elderly. They usually don't have cars and don't get around anymore. They seem to have lost interest in other people and in what's going on in the world. And other people have lost interest in them.

Me: So you deliver food to them?

Rena: Yes. With the help of gifts from stores, Clyde and I were sort of "God's delivery boys." They called our VW bus "The Love Wagon." We had fun knowing that Christ was providing.

Me: So, how did you deliver it?

Rena: In some cases we visited the people. Some were awake early in the morning. For others we left food at the door. Over a period of time they found out who was doing it. Sometimes we would leave a leaflet from the church. We learned what food people liked and needed—what doctors had told them they needed. In God's wonderful way, we always had what was needed—not an overabundance but always enough.

Me: So you gave food, your time, your energy to many lonely people. How about conversation? Did you talk with them?

Rena: To some. If we knew they needed help, we would go back in the afternoon. Some days I spent all day— starting early, delivering food, and then if a person had a special need, like needing their hair washed or needing someone to talk to, then I would go back. Mostly they wanted somebody to listen to them and share common interests with them, so their days were filled with something besides loneliness.

Me: What do you think made those people so lonely?

Rena: Many were separated from family. Most seemed to have been close to their children or their kinspeople at one time, but as they aged they got more closed in to themselves. They weren't reaching out, unless I could get them interested. I tried to do that. Sometimes I would take them too many things, and I'd say, "See how many people you can give some of this away to." This let them know not only that somebody was thinking about them, but also that others might feel the same way. My sharing helped them imagine that they could share too. I'd estimate that easily half of the people passed things on, even if it was only a doughnut.

Me: I imagine that some people coped with being alone better than others. Some get very lonely, and some not so lonely. What do you think made the difference?

Rena: Some stayed more interested in other people, and some stayed interested in other things. Some continued to work in their yards, even if their mate had died. Others had friends who would take them to activities. But some multiplied their loneliness by not staying clean and not keeping their homes clean. Other people lost interest in coming to visit.

Me: In a way these people drove others away. Not maliciously, but just because they seemed to lose interest in living.

Rena: Right. I tried to help them see that if they could get their house and their bodies clean, people might want to come by. Then I would call their old friends and tell them that our mutual acquaintances were trying to change. I might suggest that revisiting their friends would mean a lot.

Others had different problems. Sometimes a person would become ill and not be able to get out. Their friends after a while would stop coming by. Sometimes I would call and remind them that a visit would be important.

Me: That's a delicate thing to broach with someone. How did you help a person see that she was driving others away?

Rena: I might offer to take some of their clothing with me and wash it and bring it back. I'd let them keep their privacy and take off what they could. Then I would find something relatively fresh and let them give me whatever they like—not insisting. For example, I might say, "That blouse, I notice, needs a little sewing. I'll take it and mend it and get it right back to you in a couple of days." Then I would make a definite point to be fast to get the things back. I would do the same thing over and over again. I tried not to destroy their dignity or their privacy. Many of the people had a great deal of pride. They had lost some of it because they had lost interest in life.

With some people, I would help clean their house. I would try to get them to do it with me. When it came to washing their clothes or trying to get their hair clean or their body, I'd do as much as I could without embarrassing them. Then I'd give them a cloth. I usually had to initiate it. Many are over eighty. For some, it was hard for them even to remember some of the things they needed to do. I could always let them fix me coffee. I would be a guest in *their* house. In this way they could accept some of the help I gave. At first, I would tread lightly, because loneliness is very delicate. People feel deserted, as if others don't care, even though some do.

Me: Can you think of some other times that you've been able to help someone who was lonely?

Rena: Some women have little children. They don't always recognize that they are lonely because they are busy. I found that if I would stop by and spend some time talking with them, they would say, "Oh, if you only

knew how much I needed someone to talk to. I only
have little ones to talk to all day." In a way, those young
mothers are lonely. But I've found that I can't just go
to visit them. I usually pitch in and help, because they
are so busy that they would get more behind if they
stopped to just talk. There are always little people running around. I get busy with them. I usually see four
or five young mothers each week. . . . When we try to
face loneliness with someone else, I think we have to
be willing to give a lot of ourselves. There is no way
to help otherwise. Loneliness requires a lot of giving
because lonely people need to absorb a lot of taking
before they can start giving to others. That is the most
rewarding part of helping, though—to see them share
with someone else. Right away loneliness lessens. It
doesn't necessarily disappear, but it lessens.

12

HELPING IN A CRISIS

A crisis is a critical situation in which a decision is required. In crises people often think a decision must be immediate, and they are often unable or unwilling to make that decision. So they turn for help—to you.

What you do will probably depend on your knowledge of how people in crisis behave and on how you react in emotionally charged, pressure-filled situations. You will be of more help if you have a plan. This chapter will look at how people act during crises and will provide a general plan for helping in a crisis.

Almost any situation can become a crisis since a crisis is a matter of perspective. So even if it does not seem like a crisis to us, we must treat it like a crisis if that is what the person seeking help thinks it is. Of course, some situations often are crises—discovering disease, dealing with permanent injury, discovering one's own approaching death, fearing mental disorder ("nervous breakdown"), dealing with rape, deciding to drop out of school, giving up the faith, contemplating suicide, changing careers or jobs, getting a separation or divorce. These situations have something in common: they require an apparently irrevocable and important decision. Decisions imply conflicts between choices, and people in conflict feel fluctuating urges to withdraw, vacillate or merely not decide.

Crises usually begin abruptly. Because of the surprise, people are not prepared to make the important decision. They slide into negative emotions. Typically, people can see no positive resolutions. They see only the problem and cannot hear suggestions for help. They become vulnerable, needing the support and presence of another.

People in crises are usually highly emotional. They cry; they are frustrated, angry and often terrified of making a decision. Strong emotion replaces clear thinking. People concentrate on the limited time they have to make their decision. Although they feel pressured to act, their thinking becomes "channelized"; they feel that each option is like a tunnel—as if once they enter the tunnel there is no exit. They concentrate on the few alternatives they think they have, or on all the terrible things that might happen. Usually these thoughts begin with the words *What if?* "What if I die? What will my family do then?" Or, "What if she leaves me?"

How do we respond when someone comes to us in crisis? Usually two thoughts predominate. First, we might feel inadequate and afraid. "What if he loses control? What if I can't help him? I've never done this before. I feel like I'm out of my depth. He will probably kill himself," and so on. Second, we might feel an overwhelming responsibility to help. "If I can't help, she'll go crazy. I must do something. She can't function alone. What can I do now?" and so on. Thus we may be feeling two conflicting messages: I must help but I can't.

In short, we are confused. We have a choice: we can either join the panic or we can choose to work to solve the problems. Think something like, "Okay, hold it. I'm confused. That means I'm in conflict. Let me see if I can untangle this confusion. Calm down;

slow down. First, I must get my mind off me and onto the problem at hand. Exactly what is this person telling me that the problem is? What kind of alternatives are there?"

Once we have control of ourselves, we can concentrate better on the person in crisis. What is he or she saying? What started this crisis? By understanding the person and the crisis, we can begin to make useful suggestions for managing the crisis.

Marge and Harry

Marge called Ruth and asked if she could visit and talk over something that is bothering her.[1] Ruth agreed. As soon as Marge walked in, she began crying hysterically. Three times she tried to tell Ruth what the trouble is. Each time she mentions Harry's name, she begins to sob again. Her sobs are becoming less frequent, and Ruth senses that she is ready to try to talk again.

(Pretend you are Ruth. Cover each sentence with a piece of paper until you have determined what you would say. Then compare your response with Ruth's.)

Ruth: Okay, Marge, before you say anything, how about taking a deep breath? Good. I want to help, but I need to know what has happened. Now, it has to do with Harry, right? (She nods.) When did it happen?

Marge: This morning. Last year. Who knows when it happened? All I know is I've lost him.

Ruth: Lost him? (Puzzled)

Marge: Yeah. He left. This morning. He just walked into breakfast like usual and announced that he was moving out. Moving out. Just like that. (She snaps her fingers, then pauses.)

Ruth: (Silence, waiting)

Marge: Said he was moving into an apartment in town. (Pause) He told me that he couldn't take it anymore. (Pause)

Ruth: Couldn't take what?

Marge: Our arguing, I guess. See, we've been having these terrible arguments periodically over the last year or so.

Just three days ago we had another one—a real door-slammer. I guess that made him move out. He said he had already made the arrangements for an apartment, and that he would pick up the rest of his clothes and stuff tonight.

Ruth: This argument, what was it about? If you don't mind talking about it.

Marge: It was just like all the others. About his nagging me. He always nags me to do all these little, unimportant things.

Ruth: Sounds like you're angry about that.

Marge: Yeah. If it were important, I could maybe understand. But no. It's pick up this. Wash the dishes. Don't watch so much TV. Where does he get off nagging me about TV? He just reads all the time, and I never nag him. I don't watch TV half as much as he nags.

Ruth: I imagine it gets tiring to be nagged.

Marge: I guess he felt justified in leaving because he was tired of the arguing.

Ruth: Oh?

Marge: Yeah. You see, he complained about my . . . uh . . . well, my sex drive is not as high as his, and . . .

Ruth: So you two have had some arguments about how often to make love?

Marge: Yeah. He puts a lot of pressure on me. I haven't enjoyed making love for at least six months. Oh, I hope he's not having an affair! I've tried to be a good wife, but . . . well, sex with him just isn't like in the movies. I just don't know what to do.

Ruth: So you think that he nags too much and also puts too much pressure on you for sex. And he complains that your sex drive is too low.

Marge: Yeah. That's most of it. Of course, sex just isn't much fun anymore.

Ruth: Well, Marge, what are you going to do?

Marge: I don't know. Just wait for him to call, I guess. What if
            he asks for a divorce? I don't know how I can face my
            parents if we get divorced. They told me not to marry
            Harry. They'll say "I told you so," and I know I'll feel
            like a little girl again. And church. Oh, I'll never be able
            to show my face. God hates divorce, and everybody at
            church thinks divorce is a sin. This is terrible.

Ruth: Marge, has Harry mentioned divorce?

Marge: Well, not really.

Ruth: But you think that he'd like to ask for a divorce.

Marge: I don't know. He said he loved me this morning. But
            I don't know.

Ruth: What other options do you have besides just waiting
            for Harry to make the first move?

Marge: Well, I guess I could talk with the pastor. He does
            marriage counseling. Maybe he would see Harry and
            me.

Ruth: How do you think Harry would react to that?

Marge: I don't know. He might go along.

Ruth: What are you going to do about the sex problem? Is
            the pastor trained to counsel you about that?

Marge: He might be. But if he isn't, I do know of a physician
            who works with couples having sexual problems. I'll
            bet I could get an appointment with her.

Ruth: Sounds like you have some constructive things you can
            do. What do you intend to do when you leave here?

Marge: Well, I'm going to call the pastor, and then if he can't
            help with the sex thing, I'll call Dr. Smith.

Ruth: There's one other thing I would like us to do before
            you leave, Marge. Can we pray about this problem?
            God created marriage, and he can surely heal it.

Marge: Thanks. Let's do pray.

In this example, things went smoothly. Things are usually not
so smooth in real life! Ruth behaved in a number of effective
ways. Let's review some of them.

Steps in Crisis Helping

1. Quiet the person. Crises are emotional times. Strong emotion is like an alarm clock on a tin tub. It gets our attention. How can we get people's minds off their emotion? We can try to change their bodily responses and their thinking. Here's how.

☐ Have them sit down if they are not already sitting.

☐ Have them take a deep breath.

☐ Reassure them that you are there and willing to listen and help.

☐ Speak more softly than they do.

☐ Speak slowly—space your sentences.

☐ Be firm.

☐ Be explicit.

☐ Ask a question that requires a short response, such as yes or no.

☐ Ask, at first, questions that are concrete. As the person calms down, ask questions requiring longer answers.

2. Listen to the person. Try to understand what the person is saying, doing and thinking. At first, steer clear of what the person is feeling, especially if the person is emotional. Listen actively to understand the problem.

3. Evaluate. What does the person want to accomplish? What does the person want you to do? Can you do it? You cannot solve long-term problems during a crisis. Don't try. Concentrate on the emergency. Emergency implies something NEW and NOW *emerging.* What is new? What can be done about it? In crisis situations, be more interested in what the person can do NOW than in how they got in this predicament.

4. Help the person explore alternatives. The person may have thought more about the alternatives than you. Chances are, however, that the crisis has focused his or her thinking on one or two alternatives and on catastrophic consequences for each. So help the person break out of the prison of restricted thinking. Here are several ways to do this.

☐ Ask, "What can you do to help yourself?"

☐ Ask, "What other alternatives have you already considered?"

☐ Brainstorm. Brainstorming is a technique often useful for thinking up alternatives. The rules of brainstorming are as follows: (a) Set a limited time period. (b) Mention alternatives without regard to how practical they are. Emphasize quantity and originality of suggestions rather than quality. (c) Write down each alternative as it is mentioned. (d) At the end of the time period set aside for brainstorming, investigate each alternative.

☐ Suggest alternatives. If all else has failed, *you* make suggestions. People seem to be more likely to use a suggestion if they make it themselves. Give them as much chance as possible to do this before you make suggestions.

As the person names alternatives, help him or her to evaluate how likely the event is and what the consequences might be if it occurs. Sometimes you can help people consider their strengths and determine how they will employ their strengths to solve their problems.

5. Develop an action plan. As the person explores alternatives, determine what steps must be taken to move the person out of crisis. Help the person set goals and decide what order to accomplish them. Stress the actions that will accomplish goals rather than the goals themselves. Help the person decide in what order to perform the actions.

6. Have the person repeat the plan of action. When the person has a definite plan for action, ask, "What will you do when you leave here?" By having the person repeat the plan, you accomplish two important things—you assure yourself that he or she does have a plan, and you help the person "own" the plan, increasing the chances he or she will carry it out.

7. Follow up after the talk. Once you have helped the person through a crisis, follow up on whether the person resolved the problem that precipitated the crisis. Be available for additional help or refer the person to someone who can give the help the person still needs. Your continued follow-up will show that you really care for the person; it conveys Christian love. It might also

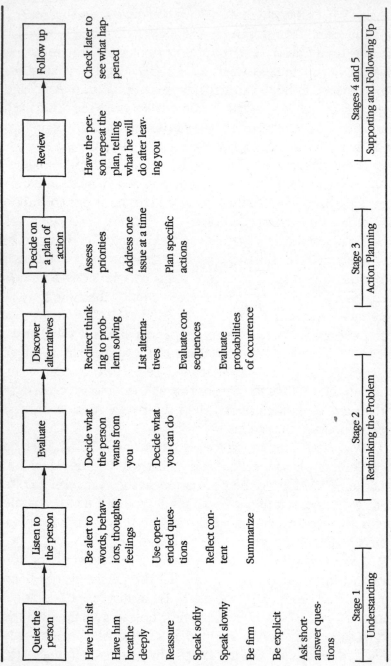

Figure 8.   Helping in Crisis

provide opportunities for long-term helping or, if you had been previously involved with long-term helping for the person, this might strengthen your relationship with the person and give him or her increased confidence in your ability to help.

The steps to follow in crisis helping are really the same five stages of helping we have suggested throughout (see figure 8). Although it is a condensed version, we can never short-cut listening and understanding as the basis for rethinking and action planning. As with any helping ministry, we need to remain humble. We must respect our pastor, our spouse and our friend. As we rely on God, he will make us his usable vessels.

13

THINE IS
THE POWER

If counseling is new to you, you probably feel both enthusiastic to try some of these ideas and afraid of what will happen if you do. I wanted to inspire you to improve your skill at helping, to develop a confident feeling that you can talk to someone struggling with self issues, fear, depression or loneliness. You *can* help. You now have some new ways to think about these problems and new action plans to recommend if God calls you to help.

In terms of the five-step model I have proposed, this book has concentrated on stages two and three. Stage one (understanding the person and communicating that understanding) is probably the most important part of lay helping. *When Someone Asks for Help* dealt with those skills. But helping is more than understanding. People need to rethink their problem in a way that offers hope of a solution. This is stage two. The goal of stage three is to develop an action plan that can free people from their emotional bonds. Here we want to be creative, unafraid to experiment, and help people try many ways of solving their problem. Not every plan will work for every person. In fact, people might try many plans before hitting on the one that finally dislodges them from their emotional mire. Support and follow-up (stages four and five) were not covered in detail but are crucial. They confirm our commitment to individuals and our willingness to lay down our life for them.

For an easy reference to helping people with particular problems, the Appendix that follows offers in brief, tabular form the steps to take in dealing with problems of the self, fear, depression and loneliness.

The Gift of Helping

God gives gifts to his church. When part of Christ's body is in pain, he raises up another part to ease that pain. If he has chosen any of us to help, he expects us to take responsible action. All of us, at one time or another, minister to our "siblings" in the Lord. We cannot complacently wait for the elders, the pastor or even Christian professionals to counsel those wounded in spirit or emotion. God certainly works through each of these, but the Bible teaches that he uses the *whole* body in growing his people.

In my experience, we rarely if ever feel adequate to the task. If we do feel adequate, God has a way of opening our eyes (Prov 16:18). Even though I have counseled many people, both professionally and as a friend, I still am excited and unsure of what the Lord is bringing across my path each time I begin to help. At one time I had several clients who successfully conquered depression. I must admit to feeling quite smug about my skill at helping them. Then the Lord sent me another woman with whom I tried my proven counseling strategies. Instead of getting better, she got worse. When she finally hospitalized herself for depression, I was ready to join her. God got my attention and snapped me out of my prideful complacency. Now I look at each new client as a reminder to rely on God—not myself, not my techniques. Cautious of my attitude and my limits, I can yet act confidently in my Lord.

Bearing this same attitude, we can all help others. Let's review the process. First, assess whether you are able to provide the help that people are seeking from you. If not, refer them to someone who can. You'll want to have handy a list of professionals in your area for quick reference. When you do refer people to a counselor, then focus your effort on understanding and supporting them as they change.

If you decide, on the other hand, to try to help the person yourself, take time to determine how. Read, study, think and pray about the person and the problem. Analyze your motives in helping. Who are you hoping to build up—the other person or yourself? When you discover self-aggrandizement as a motive, ask forgiveness and bring that motive under the blood of Jesus. Then help the other person. After the cleansing of forgiveness, it is counterproductive to continue to search your motives. Rather, focus on the other person, promote his or her welfare, and your motives will soon take care of themselves.

Helpers are like guides on a big-game hunt. They lead people to the place where they can slay the monsters that plague them. Unfortunately, as guides, we cannot promise success. All we can do is use our knowledge of the terrain and of how the monsters usually act to point out some probable routes to the game. Nor can we promise that the going will be easy. Dense jungle foliage may have to be hacked through, and we may not have a machete large enough to do the job without a struggle. But there is comfort in knowing that the God of our gardens is also Lord of the jungle.

The heaviest work is done by those seeking help. Usually they feel stuck or paralyzed. While we may help release them from the glue that binds them, *they* elect to move. They decide what to do. They carry out the decisions. They experiment. They feel the consequences in their lives.

Helpers cannot be overly concerned with making a mistake. If we make a recommendation that they do not like, they will tell us. Our recommendations are just that. They must be tested by others to see whether they are appropriate. If we make numerous suggestions and people don't act on them, we must treat this as their choice. Anger is out of place. Rather, it's time to stop making suggestions and to ask what *they* would like to do to solve their problem. Here we confess our inability to solve the problem and redouble our effort to understand them. We increase our prayers.

People often know what they need to do to get over an emotional problem. They just have trouble doing it. Our task is to encourage them—to help them have courage—and to stick by them as they courageously try to change. Their job is to seek the Lord and to try to do whatever he says.

God, the Wonderful Counselor

The Holy Spirit is always active when God's people are struggling to grow. He comforts them in their suffering. He readies them to understand what they must do to find relief from their problems. Then he leads them to understanding. He convicts of sin. He confronts them and prompts them to act. Finally, the Holy Spirit empowers the person to carry out his promptings.

Jesus' finished work on the cross gives our life meaning and provides the basis of all healing. Sometimes this healing comes dramatically and immediately. Other times people must wait for healing. Jesus has laid up an inheritance for us in heaven, and he gives us installments on the way (see Eph 1:3-14). Total healing and everlasting health are awaiting us, for "by his wounds [we] have been healed" (1 Pet 2:24). Yet we must not, like the prodigal son, claim our inheritance before the proper time (Lk 15:11-32). We are to live now under our Father's care, enjoying the benefits he daily provides. "We are children of God, and if children, then heirs, heirs of God and fellow heirs with Christ, provided we suffer with him in order that we may also be glorified with him" (Rom 8:16-17).

If someone is to be healed, Jesus will do it. He hears us when we pray, and he carries our prayers to the Father. He might use us to bring about the healing. He sometimes lets us participate in seeing him work. Joy is our reward for responsible helping. But he is the healer. By his wounds we have been healed.

God the Father is the source of all good things. We seek his will, and he will have his way. His mercy saves people that we help from what they deserve, just as it rescues us. His grace provides good things they don't deserve. He is sovereign. Jesus prayed, "Thy kingdom come, Thy will be done, On earth as it is in heaven" (Mt 6:10). He is the King of the kingdom. We are his subjects and so are those we help. They are in his hands, and he will care for them. We can do nothing apart from him. The power to deliver is his.

As we set out to help, we begin and end by affirming what we know: "For thine is the kingdom and the power and the glory, for ever. Amen."

Appendix

A Ready Summary of Action Plans

Rethink the Problem	ACTION PLANS		
	Change Behaviors	Change Thoughts	Change Environment
Self-concepts are rational beliefs; self-images are nonrational and pictorial; self-esteem is emotional evaluation of self. There are original causes (such as rejection) and current causes. Only Jesus heals the original. You can help them change current causes. Assess which current causes are concerned with actions, which with beliefs, and which with circumstances (A-B-C).	1. Pray for healing of rejection (if present). 2. Help them forgive the one who rejected and repent of their own bitterness. 3. Help them change social skills that drive friends away. 4. Help them stop procrastinating. 5. Help them get rid of persistent sin. 6. Help them praise God for their problems. 7. Encourage prayer. 8. Help them adopt a role of their ideal self and act it for three weeks. 9. Help them deal with persistent failure. 10. Help them conduct spiritual warfare.	1. Indoctrinate self in who we are in Christ. 2. Change misunderstandings. 3. Change distorted ways of thinking, rigid thinking, twisting evidence, negative self-indoctrination. 4. Change destructive metaphors to healing metaphors. 5. Use fantasies to reach the self-image. 6. Combat the belief that changing negative thinking won't work by challenging the person to give it a longer test. 7. Combat the argument that this method is artificial by agreeing that the method is artificial (but insisting that it still helps healing, like a cast on a broken arm). 8. Add to the self-image or modify it. Then practice the new image intentionally. 9. Or, create an entirely new self-image and practice it systematically.	Get them to associate more with uncritical, affirming people.

Table 1. Helping People Change the Self

	ACTION PLANS		
Rethink the Problem	**Change Behaviors**	**Change Thoughts**	**Change Environment**
1. Old self versus new self; to which will we yield? **2.** God fights our battles if we discern and follow his leading. **3.** Self-control involves many daily decisions; it is not a personality trait. **4.** Self-control is a problem for all of us; the area we find difficult varies. There is no room for judging another.	**1.** Help them add short-term and long-term rewards for self-control. **2.** Get them to enter a relationship in which they are accountable for self-control or lack of it. **3.** Take into account that everyone fails at some time. Don't give up after a failure. **4.** Help them make long-term consequences more immediate. **5.** Pray that God will reveal a way out of temptation. Listen for his answer. **6.** Interrupt the normal chain of events, at several points if possible.	**1.** Encourage them to glorify God. **2.** Help them build an edifying thought life. **3.** In each self-control situation, ask self, "How can I meet this challenge in a way that will glorify God?" **4.** Plan ahead how they will handle difficult decision points. **5.** Share some of the ways that you handle difficulties in self-control, while cautioning them that the ways might not work for them. **6.** Replace negative fantasies with more positive (or at least different) fantasies. **7.** Suggest mental diversion.	**1.** Suggest they avoid situations in which temptation might occur. **2.** Get temptations out of their sight. **3.** Help change the physical cues in the temptation situation. **4.** Suggest some visual cue that will remind them to practice self-control. Warning: Cues must be changed frequently because people begin to ignore them.

Table 2. Helping People Gain Self-Control

Rethink the Problem	ACTION PLANS		
	Change Behaviors	Change Thoughts	Change Environment
1. Fear and anxiety are both due to anticipating harmful consequences of some behavior. **2.** Fear is due to our appraisal of a situation as threatening; our bodies react to the threat. **3.** Worry triggers fear, which feeds on itself. **4.** Determine if they have created unnecessary anxiety by overgeneralization from disturbing events. **5.** Beware of offering common-sense suggestions. Most people have tried these and have not been helped. **6.** The antidote to fear is to trust in God.	**1.** Check to see whether they have tried the common-sense solutions to fear (see pp. 79-80): a. Physical avoidance b. Attention diversion c. Analysis **2.** Look up relevant Scripture verses (see p. 81). **3.** Analyze fear logically. Determine the real probability that the feared consequence will occur.	**1.** Help them fear the Lord: a. Praise him b. Trust him c. Bless him d. Serve him **2.** Help them hate evil and depart from evil. **3.** Pray that God will give them a new vision to replace fearful imagery. **4.** Help them create a new image.	Suggest that they avoid the fearful situation.

Table 3. Helping People Who Are Anxious or Fearful

	ACTION PLANS		
Rethink the Problem	Change Habits	Change Thoughts	Change Environment
1. What kind of obstacle are they blocked by—unavoidable events or unrealistic goals?	**1.** Help them get daily tasks done.	**1.** Help them realize:	**1.** Seek prayer from the elders of your church (see Jas 5:13-16).
2. How has their depression made their pressures worse?	**2.** Have them make a list of things to do and cross off each as done.	a. Even if they don't have control, God does.	**2.** Have them arrange their surroundings so they are orderly, bright and cheerful.
3. How can they regain control of the situation?	**3.** Suggest they do something fun, not eliminate all the positive feelings in life.	b. Our thoughts control our emotions.	**3.** Have them avoid near-certain failure situations if possible.
4. What small, short-range goal could they handle?	**4.** Pray for healing.	c. We must consciously change our thinking. It will soon become "automatic."	
5. What kind of negative thinking are they doing?	**5.** Suggest exercise	d. We must work continually to change our thinking.	
	6. Study Psalm 42 together.	**2.** Explain how to change thoughts:	
		a. Don't tell yourself, "Don't be depressed"; rather, get your mind off yourself.	
		b. Don't just repeat the same message; reason with yourself.	
		c. Plan specific thoughts to help anticipate depressing situations, confront the first signs of depression, and handle full-blown depression.	
		3. Remember what God has done for you and encourage them to do the same.	
		4. Get them to actively question their depression.	

Table 4. Helping People Who Are Depressed

	ACTION PLANS		
Rethink the Problem	**Change Behaviors**	**Change Thoughts**	**Change Environment**
1. Loneliness is a result of three problems: a. Not completely trusting God. b. Social aloneness and isolation. c. Self-preoccupation, rigidity and rejection. **2.** Work on all problems simultaneously. **3.** Careful groundwork must be laid by listening and assessing what can be done: a. How God wants you to help. b. Whether lack of social contact or lack of intimacy is the problem. c. Possible causes of loneliness. d. Whether depression and anxiety are present and if so, to what degree. **4.** Beware being attached to your conceptualization of the problem.	**1.** Build the faith of the lonely by allowing God to work in your life, then talking about it to them. **2.** Examine how they provoke others to reject them. **3.** Put ideas that seem illogical to the test. Have them experiment. **4.** Help them restructure their time schedule. Often little changes produce big results.	**1.** Loneliness is a gift from God that motivates relationships. **2.** Loneliness is a problem to solve. It is a time to work out faith through action—not to wait for a rescue by someone else. **3.** Move them away from feeling sorry for themselves or thinking life is unfair.	**1.** Help with practical tasks: a. Cleaning. b. Clothes repair and washing. c. Household chores. **2.** Give the lonely a reason to reach out to others. **3.** Meet the practical needs of the lonely in terms of finances, transportation, assistance and fellowship. **4.** Offer to give them a ride to church functions.

Table 5. Helping People Who Are Lonely

Notes

Chapter 1: Who, Me? Help Others?
[1]These five steps are described more fully in my earlier book *When Someone Asks for Help* (Downers Grove, Ill.: InterVarsity Press, 1982).
[2]Robert Carkhuff, "Differential Functioning of Lay and Professional Helpers," *Journal of Counseling Psychology* 15 (1968): 117; A. Hoffman and R. Warmer, "Paraprofessional Effectiveness," *Personnel and Guidance Journal* 54 (1976): 494-97.
[3]W. F. Brown, "Effectiveness of Paraprofessionals: The Evidence," *Personnel and Guidance Journal* 53 (1974): 257-63.

Chapter 2: I'm Just a Toad
[1]Earl Jabay, *Search for Identity: A View of Authentic Christian Living* (Grand Rapids: Zondervan, 1967); *The Kingdom of Self* (Plainfield, N.J.: Logos International, 1974).
[2]Josh McDowell, *His Image, My Image* (San Bernardino: Here's Life Publishers, Inc., 1984); Earl D. Wilson, *The Undivided Self: Bringing Your Whole Life in Line with God's Will* (Downers Grove, Ill.: InterVarsity Press, 1983).
[3]David G. Myers, "A New Look at Pride," in Craig W. Ellison, ed., *Your Better Self: Christianity, Psychology and Self-Esteem* (San Francisco: Harper & Row/CAPS Book, 1983), pp. 82-97.
[4]Craig W. Ellison, "Self-esteem: An Overview," in Ellison, *Your Better Self*, pp. 1-20.
[5]Peter Marshall, "Morning Glory," in *Mr. Jones, Meet the Master: Sermons and*

Prayers of Peter Marshall (Richmond: John Knox Press, 1949), p. 186.
[6]Claude Steiner, *Scripts People Live: Transactional Analysis of Life Scripts* (New York: Bantam, 1975).

Chapter 3: Improving Self-Image
[1]Ruth Carter Stapleton, *The Gift of Inner Healing* (Waco, Tex.: Word Books, 1976).
[2]For examples of how to do this see Don Meichenbaum, *Cognitive-Behavior Modification: An Integrative Approach* (New York: Plenum, 1977).
[3]Peter J. Lang, "Imagery in Therapy: An Information Processing Analysis of Fear," *Behavior Therapy* 8 (1977): 862-86.
[4]Ann Kiemel, *I'm Out to Change My World* (Nashville: Impact Books, 1974).
[5]George A. Kelly, *The Psychology of Personal Constructs,* vols. 1 & 2 (New York: Norton, 1955). See also Martin Bolt and David G. Myers, "Behavior and Belief," in *The Human Connection* (Downers Grove, Ill.: InterVarsity Press, 1984).

Chapter 4: Wanted: Self-Control
[1]Paul W. Clement, "Self-regulation and Self-esteem," in Craig W. Ellison, ed., *Your Better Self: Christianity, Psychology and Self-Esteem* (San Francisco: Harper & Row/CAPS Book, 1983), pp. 111-21; C. E. Thoreson and M. J. Mahoney, *Behavioral Self-control* (New York: Holt, Rinehart and Winston, 1974); M. J. Mahoney and C. E. Thoreson, eds., *Self-control: Power to the Person* (Monterey, Calif.: Brooks/Cole, 1973); D. L. Watson and R. G. Tharp, *Self-directed Behavior: Self-modification for Personal Adjustment,* 2d ed. (Monterey, Calif.: Brooks/Cole, 1977).
[2]F. H. Kanfer, "The Many Faces of Self-Control, or Behavior Modification Changes Its Focus," in R. B. Stuart, ed., *Behavioral Self-management: Strategies, Techniques and Outcomes* (New York: Brunner/Mazel, 1977).

Chapter 5: Winning the Battle for Self-Control
[1]John White, *The Fight: A Practical Handbook for Christian Living* (Downers Grove, Ill.: InterVarsity Press, 1976).
[2]Walter Mischel and B. Moore, "Effects of Attention to Symbolically Presented Rewards on Self-Control," *Journal of Personality and Social Psychology* 34 (1976): 419-24.

Chapter 6: The Tyranny of Fear
[1]Richard Morris, "Fear Reduction Methods," in Frederick H. Kanfer and Arnold P. Goldstein, eds., *Helping People Change,* 2d ed. (New York: Pergamon, 1980), pp. 248-93.
[2]Ibid., pp. 248-49.

Chapter 7: Calming the Fearful
[1]See Prov 10:24; Is 54:14; Mt 10:31; 1 Pet 3:6, 13-15; 1 Jn 4:16-18.

²See also, for high-level fear, Matthew 10:26-31 and John 4:16-18, which were too lengthy to quote.
³Joseph Wolpe, *Psychotherapy by Reciprocal Inhibition* (Stanford, Calif.: Stanford University Press, 1958).
⁴Meichenbaum, *Cognitive-Behavior Modification.*
⁵Morris, "Fear Reduction Methods," pp. 277-83.
⁶Ps 27:1; 46:1-2; 56:3-4; 118:6; Prov 29:25; Mt 6:25-34; Phil 4:6-7.

Chapter 8: Depression: A Downward Spiral
¹Martin E. P. Seligman, *Helplessness: On Depression, Development, and Death* (San Francisco: Freeman, 1975).
²*Journal of Abnormal Psychology* (special issue on learned helplessness as a model of depression) 87 (1978).
³Lynn Y. Abramson and Martin E. P. Seligman, "Learned Helplessness in Humans: Critique and Reformulation," *Journal of Abnormal Psychology* 87 (1978): 49-74.
⁴Aaron T. Beck, *Cognitive Therapy and the Emotional Disorders* (New York: International Universities Press, 1976).

Chapter 9: Helping the Depressed
¹D. Martyn Lloyd-Jones, *Spiritual Depression: Its Causes and Cure* (Grand Rapids: William B. Eerdmans, 1965), p. 20.
²D. R. Pecheur and K. J. Edwards, "A Comparison of Secular and Religious Versions of Cognitive Therapy with Depressed Christian College Students," *Journal of Psychology and Theology* 12 (1984): 45-54; L. R. Propst, "A Comparison of the Cognitive Restructuring Psychotherapy Paradigm and Several Spiritual Approaches to Mental Health," *Journal of Psychology and Theology* 8 (1980):107-14.
³John White, *The Masks of Melancholy: A Christian Physician Looks at Depression and Suicide* (Downers Grove, Ill.: InterVarsity Press, 1982).

Chapter 10: The Pain of Loneliness
¹C. Rubenstein, P. Shaver, and L. A. Peplau, "Loneliness," *Human Nature* 2 (1970): 58-65.
²L. A. Peplau and D. Perlman, eds., *Loneliness: A Sourcebook of Current Theory, Research and Therapy* (New York: John Wiley & Sons, 1982), p. 5.
³R. Weiss, *Loneliness: The Experiences of Emotional and Social Isolation* (Cambridge, Mass.: MIT Press, 1973).
⁴Janice G. Williams and Cecilia H. Solano, "The Social Reality of Feeling Lonely," *Personality and Social Psychology Bulletin* 9 (1983): 237-42.
⁵Cecilia H. Solano, Phillip G. Batten and Elizabeth A. Parish, "Loneliness and Patterns of Self-Disclosure," *Journal of Personality and Social Psychology* 43 (1982): 545-51.
⁶R. A. Goswick and W. H. Jones, "Loneliness, Self-Concept, and Adjustment,"

Journal of Psychology 107 (1981): 237-40; W. H. Jones, S. A. Hobbs, and D. Hockenbury, "Loneliness and Social Skills Deficits," *Journal of Personality and Social Psychology* 42 (1982): 682-89.

⁷William W. Sloan, Jr., and Cecilia H. Solano, "The Conversational Styles of Lonely Males with Strangers and Roommates," *Personality and Social Psychology Bulletin* 10 (1984): 293-301.

⁸Goswick and Jones, "Loneliness, Self-Concept, and Adjustment," pp. 237-40; W. H. Jones, J. E. Freemon, and R. A. Goswick, "The Persistence of Loneliness: Self and Other Determinants," *Journal of Personality* 49 (1981): 27-48; Jones, Hobbs, and Hockenbury, "Loneliness and Social Skills Deficits," pp. 682-89; Sloan and Solano, "Conversational Styles," pp. 293-301.

⁹Paul Tournier, *Escape from Loneliness,* trans. John S. Gilmour (Philadelphia: Westminster Press, 1962), p. 31.

¹⁰Keith Miller and Bruce Larson, *Living the Adventure: Faith and "Hidden" Difficulties* (Waco, Tex.: Word Books, 1975), pp. 45-62.

¹¹Tournier, *Escape from Loneliness,* pp. 159-89.

Chapter 11: Defeating Loneliness
¹H. J. Strupp, S. W. Hadley, and B. Gomez-Schwartz, *Psychotherapy for Better or Worse* (New York: Jason Aronson, 1977).

²Miller and Larson, *Living the Adventure,* p. 23.